BEING A BOY

JAMES DAWSON

with illustrations by Spike Gerrell

RED LEMON PRESS

FOR MUM

First published in Great Britain by Red Lemon Press Limited
Northburgh House, 10 Northburgh Street, London EC1V 0AT, UK

Text copyright © 2013 James Dawson
Illustration copyright © 2013 Spike Gerrell

ISBN 978-1-7834-2000-1
A CIP catalogue record for this book is available from the
British Library.

Printed and bound by Clays Ltd, St Ives Plc

FSC

Red Lemon Press supports the Forest Stewardship Council (FSC), the leading international
forest certification organisation, and is commited to printing on Greenpeace-approved
FSC-certified paper where possible.

1 3 5 7 9 8 6 4 2

www.redlemonpress.com

Cover design by Katie Knutton

Red Lemon Press Limited is part of the Bonnier Publishing Group
www.bonnierpublishing.com

CONTENTS

1. Being a boy   5
2. The new alpha male   17
3. Looking good   37
4. Pubes and sex stuff   59
5. Always wear a condom   113
6. Being a boyfriend   129
7. Being a man   173
8. The school dictionary   180
9. Helpful numbers and stuff   185
10. Being a grown-up   187
11. About the author   192

CHAPTER 1

BEING A BOY

BEING A BOY IS HARD

It's harder to be a girl because they have to push enormous babies out of a very small hole and also because we live in a pretty sexist world run almost exclusively by rich men.

Putting that to one side, it's still really hard to be a boy. In some ways it's harder than being a girl because, unlike boys, girls are encouraged to share and talk about their problems, for the most part.

In fact to the male outsider, when girls go through puberty, they are apparently inducted into what seems to be a secret sorority – the mysterious 'clubhouse' of womanhood that men cannot enter, because we do not have periods. That's fine – by the way, if your bits are bleeding, you must see a doctor NOW – but the sad fact is, that there isn't a similar 'club' for boys where we can talk about our worries and about our bodies. For girls, it's okay to share these things in glossy magazines and chat about them in online forums or at sleepovers. But, as it is generally assumed that boys are tough and don't have emotions you may feel that you are rather left to fend for yourself.

You are about to enter, or already are within, a super-weird time in your life. EVERYTHING is about to change both inside as your body tumbles through puberty, and out, as your relationships take on a sexyfun new twist. While many girls are able to guide each other through this minefield, boys are often programmed from an early age to be STRONG and TOUGH and HARD, so we don't really talk about these changes.

Sadly, it is pretty much what society expects of boys. Sitting down and having a long conversation about what's happening to your cock is likely to be interpreted in one of two ways:

1. YOU ARE GAY.
2. YOU ARE MENTALLY ILL.

You might be neither, one or both of these things, but the fact is that WHOEVER you are, your body is going through an awful lot of changes and this can be really scary. It's fine to admit this – it won't stop you being STRONG, TOUGH and HARD. In fact, speaking up, reading this book and being honest make you pretty effing brave.

Let's say you're with your chums and some loudmouth is bragging about something sexual and in your head, you're like 'what?'. But you can't say 'what do you mean?' without looking like a MASSIVE, MASSIVE VIRGIN. If you don't feel comfortable talking to any of the adults in your life, you might never find out and could end up really worrying about sex stuff. Sure, the Internet has loads of information, but it's hard to find in-amongst all the naked ladies that pop up when all you wanted to find out was if masturbation will kill you.

That said, it's possible you have a great man in your life like a dad, uncle or big brother who can guide you through the weird stuff that's

going on, but these are difficult conversations to have. It doesn't even need to be a guy. Mums, sisters, aunts and other women are pretty good at puberty chat too but no one really likes talking about pubes, anal sex, spunk, porn and the location of the clitoris – least of all your dad when he mainly just wants to wash the dishes and have a relaxing poo in peace.

With this in mind, I have set out to answer every question you might have about your body, sex and relationships. For a long time I was a teacher and I specialised in PSHCE (personal, social, health and citizenship ed) so I taught an awful lot of sex education. This experience means I no longer have ANY SHAME so am more than happy to discuss bums, willies and lady-gardens. I am also someone who was a boy and is now a man. I more or less survived this transition.

This book will hopefully act as an ice-breaker that will allow you and the adults in your life to have a frank and honest chat about sex. If you're not in a 'let's all liberally share muesli' kind of family that's also fine and, with any luck, this book will answer all those questions you were scared to ask plus a few you didn't even know you had. Hopefully, you'll think it's funny sometimes, too. Let's face it, there is nothing funnier than a penis, so we may as well laugh about it.

BOYS AND GIRLS

If you've come to this book thinking it's a manifesto of BOYS ARE BETTER THAN GIRLS, then you are sadly mistaken. There's none of that here. In fact, I pretty much think that girls and boys are EQUAL and THE SAME in nearly every way, other than a few bits of body.

Seriously – how are we different? Are women shorter than guys? No, not always. Are they smarter? No, not always. Are they stronger, braver, tidier, funnier? Are you getting the picture?

But we DO live in a rather sexist society. This sexism is pretty much baked into our world, so it's going to take YOU and your generation an awful lot of hard work to clear out the rot. Because people in suits want to SELL YOU THINGS they try to do it based on the most basic of criteria – your gender.

So from before you are even born, everything comes in pink and blue. Advertising screamed to you and your parents: 'THIS IS WHAT BOYS WANT! THIS IS WHAT BOYS LIKE!'. Before you know it, you have some things for boys: toy guns; skulls; snakes; football; murder; pirates and BLUE. While girls and their folks get bombarded with: kittens; petals; snowflakes; horses; cupcakes; ballet and PINK.

If by some quirk you happen to be one of the MILLIONS of boys who don't like the items listed then society could make you feel like a freak and you may well have to pretend you like certain things to fit in.

It's about to get complicated now. Are you sitting comfortably? We can never know if it actually *feels* different to be 'male' or 'female', but I know this – we are only 'male' because a doctor said so when we were born. You might be sitting there, reading this, thinking that you don't feel very 'male' even though you have boy bits. This is super-common, by the way.

The Gender Question

Some boys want to be girls. Some girls want to be boys. Some boys and girls do something about this and CHOOSE their gender identity, sometimes permanently with hormone treatment or surgery, sometimes temporarily. You might hear this being called 'transgender', 'trans' or 'genderqueer'.

I think this is a very brave thing to do because most of society wants you to be MALE or FEMALE and would like you to stay that way, thank you very much.

In the eyes of most people, you get only TWO options. This is why gender is so poo, because even bloody POPCORN comes in sweet, salty and butter! There is still such a terrible lack of understanding by most people of what it means to be male or female.

We're all HUMAN. What if we were just one big gang of equal humans? I think that would be much nicer. We all want the same things – happiness, warmth, love, laughter, sex, chips and ice-cream. The biological stuff is different for obvious reasons – but as you'll see later a lot of the relationship advice is identical for both boys and girls. If you are treating your female friends differently to your male friends, I'd politely suggest there is something wrong there.

> Being a boy doesn't make you superior or even that different to girls. Got that? Brilliant.

Of course, your way of being a boy will be different to the guy sitting next to you. His way will be different to the person next to him. There are infinite ways of being a boy and they are ALL okay.

SEXUAL ORIENTATION

Another big thing that is shoved down your throat from a very young age is this fact: BOYS AND GIRLS HAVE SEX. This is true, but there's more to it. There is a whole a la carte menu of sex fun to choose from. Sometimes boys have sex with boys; sometimes girls have sex with girls. Sometimes boys have sex with girls and boys; sometimes girls have sex with boys and girls. Sometimes people say 'forget it' and have sex with neither!

Sexual orientation, or sexual preference, is quite like gender in that it is a lot more fluid than you think: GAY or STRAIGHT aren't the only options. In fact these are made up labels. I don't even know who made them up. I think it's because humans LOVE labels, whether it is black and white, rich and poor, male and female and so on. We're obsessed.

Read the first paragraph of this section again. Did I use the words gay, straight or bi? No. There's no need. There are billions of people on this planet – you will find some of them sexy, so you should attempt to have sex with some of those people.

figure a

100% FANCY WOMEN

Like sexism, homophobia is pretty much ingrained in our society. Being subtly told in lots of ways by TV, films, papers, teachers, friends and family that same-sex couples are 'different' may have led you to think that men having sex with men, or women having sex with women, is weird, dirty, shameful or strange.

WELL IT'S NOT.

I'm glad we cleared that up. Depending on which study you read, something like one in every fifteen men is likely to be attracted to other men. (Whether they have sex with them or not is another matter entirely.) That's actually quite a lot. In a class of thirty-two kids, that means two are likely to be same-sex oriented.

Just because a dude has sex with another dude doesn't automatically make him gay. It's up to an individual to decide if they like that label – it's like wearing Nike or Adidas®. It's possible 'Ted' mostly likes women, but found that one guy superhot. I call it The Mars® Bar / Snickers® Continuum. Regard figure a.

100% FANCY MEN

Let's say that men are Snickers® – because they have nuts. All men will exist somewhere on that line. Men who fancy only women will be down the Mars® Bar end; men who fancy only men are down the opposite end. But there will be MILLIONS of men who are somewhere in the middle, too. I suspect a lot of men in the middle of the line DON'T have sex with other men because they think it's weird, dirty, shameful or strange, which is sad.

Hilariously, women are bombarded with pornographic images of same-sex sex. Because the rich men that rule the world find two women having sex sexy, girls are encouraged to 'experiment'. Note that when two girls kiss they aren't automatically accused of being gay.

The world is still waiting on a pop star like Justin Bieber to record a song called, 'I Kissed a Boy and I Liked It'. It's probably not gonna happen because our society is fixated on the idea of men being MANLY and a guy snogging another guy is considered GIRLY. So you see, homophobia is very closely related to sexism.

That's the last time I really need to discuss sexual preference in this book because here's another thing: it doesn't actually matter. Young men who fancy other men are having all the same heartbreaks and traumas as boys who fancy girls. Same first love, same first kiss, same first sex, same first breakups. Every word in this book is applicable to both.

HERE WE GO

So we've established that biologically-speaking you were born 'male'. Excellent. Let's get cracking. Let's talk about some pubes and winkies.

One last thing you should be aware of: we are going to talk A LOT about sex, but we're also going to talk about things called emotions.

EE-MOW-SHUN:

1. A mental state of feeling often causing physiological responses, laughter, tears, sweat or shaking.

2. Collective term for abstract nouns such as love, fear, jealousy, joy, anxiety.

3. Something Taylor Swift sings about.

4. All the 'feels'.

In many ways it's harder to talk about emotions than sex and willies because those bits are pretty funny. It's the FEELINGS about your knob and stuff that you might struggle to talk about with your mates. So let me talk about these feelings so you don't have to: Result.

CHAPTER 2

THE NEW ALPHA MALE

THE NEW ALPHA MALE

There's a guy you know. He's probably a little older than you. He might not be the best looking guy. He might not have the best body. There's something about him though. People respect him. *You* respect him. He's well liked and has few enemies. He's a people magnet. People flock to him for advice. He has a certain something. He's cool.

But how can you feel cool when you're going through the most awkward phase of your life? Let's face it, puberty is a tough old time and you might not always feel very cool. Sadly, the pubescent wasteland is a time at which you might even spend hours thinking, 'I'm not good enough'.

How can anyone feel particularly confident knowing you could wake up tomorrow with a face full of spots and a back hairier than Bigfoot's? Then throw into the mix the fact that school is more competitive than any fight club with hundreds of boys all vying for the coveted position of top dog. Luckily, even if you don't feel cool, you can FAKE it.

'Cool' is a concept that never changes and never dates. 'Cool' existed at the dawn of time when a prehistoric microorganism saw The Big Bang and said, 'oooh, cool.' From Mick Jagger to Jay-Z; from Darth Vader to Darth Maul some guys just have it. If you could buy it, I'd sell a kidney to get it. So, how can you be cool without being a tool?

THE SOCIAL ZOO

It's a jungle out there. Or more precisely a zoo. Any school is more or less a menagerie of caged animals. Think about it, there's a feeding time and everyone's desperately trying to mate.

However unlike any good zoo, in the human habitat no one has thought to separate the species into different enclosures, which leads to the sort of carnage normally reserved for the Discovery Channel. Teeth bared, survival-of-the-fittest, flailing intestines horror. If the RSPCA inspected schools, I imagine they'd shut the lot.

As with zoo animals, there is a food chain in any group of males. Observe table one.

TABLE ONE: THE PECKING ORDER

INSOUCIANT LION

Consider our pride leader. He's not bothered. He basks in the sun while lesser lions tend to his every whim. He doesn't fight if he can help it. Despite this laid-back demeanour, you wouldn't put your head in his mouth because YOU JUST WOULDN'T.

HUGELY VISIBLE EAGLE

The high flyers. 'Why can't you be more like him?' ask the mothers of lesser birds. Flash, dynamic and over-achieving. Looks like bloody hard work though. The first to start pecking at their own feathers in self-doubt.

PEA-BRAIN PEACOCK

Looks sexy, gorgeous, confident and impressive until they open their mouths and a dim-sounding HONK is emitted.

JABBERING BABOON

There are a lot of them and they are noisy. When not screaming for attention, they are flinging poo at one another. Inordinate amount of pressing arses against car windows and frequent public displays of overt sexuality.

SHITWEASELS

There is no other name for this type of animal. The shitweasel follows bigger, better animals back to their dens before eating them. Two-faced bastards. Will lie, bullshit and steal to get ahead.

CLONED SHEEP

Vast in number, but impossible to tell apart, every sheep is a similar shape, variety and colour. Move in herds, especially in times of danger. Rarely put head above the parapet, lest they end up served with mint sauce.

CLONED SHEEP

TRAGIC VOLE

However much he can try to deny it, the vole is prey for just about every animal in the zoo, including some herbivores. Think about it – in what context other than 'gets eaten by' would you discuss this creature?

STICK INSECT

You don't even know he's there.

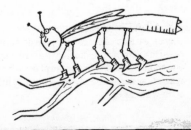

This is all in jest of course. Any of us, at any given time, will have characteristics of all of these animals and we certainly alter our behaviour in different situations. But school can bring out the worst in us, and, like it or not, there is a social hierarchy.

WILLY-WAGGLING

So, if the most aspirational position is that of insouciant lion, a rare and magnificent breed, how do we earn this rank? Well, that's the thing. When closely examining people who are truly cool, one thing is clear: They are quietly cool. Cool is as effortless as a granny slipping on an icy path. Being NOISY and cool is more in line with jabbering baboons, who are prone to 'willy-waggling'.

This term refers to hyper-masculine displays of MANLINESS. Grrrr! *pounds chest*, *eats baby*. Jabbering baboons in particular will jostle on the greasy ladder to get to the top. They will shout, banter, fight and show off. (Jabbering baboons can be witnessed on any town's high street at about 11:30 on a Friday night dragging their knuckles along a vommity pavement, kebab entrails dangling from their mouths.) In short, it's a penis parade: who is the BIGGEST, LOUDEST and STRONGEST dick in the zoo?

To an extent, willy-waggling works. If you declare your own magnificence loudly enough, you might gain a good position on the pole. But would you respect someone who gained this status through noisy thuggery? As willy-waggling is ALWAYS unpleasant to behold, perhaps what the waggler has gained is notoriety instead of cool.

Willy-waggling is a side-effect of insecurity. Observe figure b.

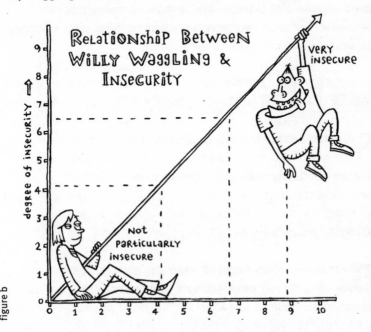

figure b

As you can see, the more insecure a person is the more prone they are to willy-waggling. Insecurity is another way of saying you are worried about being you. If you are anxious that people won't like or accept you it might make you want to willy-waggle to create a penis-shield to hide your fear. But as mentioned before, observers are more likely to say 'look at that dick.' Insecurity is not cool, and willy-waggling will make people think you are an insecure baboon.

Don't get me wrong, baboons are a brilliant and entertaining part of a zoo visit, but they are nothing compared to the lions. Insouciant lions do not need to willy-waggle. On any trip to the zoo, I have only ever seen lions lounging around in the sun but I still wouldn't go in the enclosure. The beast has my respect even though he has done nothing. Or has he?

In actual fact, the insouciant lions *are* doing something. They are doing nothing. Are you with me? By refraining from willy-waggling, they are sending out a clear message that they are secure in themselves. They like themselves therefore you should, too.

Getting people to like you starts with liking yourself.

EVERYONE HATES CHANGE ...

But change is inevitable. Being angry about the changes that are happening to your body is about as productive as shouting at the clouds on a rainy day.

That said, with so much going on puberty can be a really unsettling time. You'll welcome some of the changes, after all, who doesn't love having genitals that now feel like a furry gerbil, but some might be more problematic and cause feelings (remember we discussed feelings?) of insecurity.

The classic example are those angel-faced choirboys who can no longer hit the high notes once their balls drop. (FYI, that phrase is used a lot, but your balls don't drop very far at all. You won't be in Asda when a testicle suddenly pops out the bottom of your jeans.)

You may find your body uncooperative physically. As you get bigger you may find yourself less athletic, fast or flexible – a real worry for our high-flying eagles. You will certainly find yourself getting more tired than before as energy is redirected into growth. That said, you may also find unexpected benefits. If you suddenly shoot up to six foot five, a whole new career in basketball might open up to you.

No matter what you pull out of the puberty grab bag, all of these things are a real head trip. Imagine a caterpillar becoming a butterfly, he must be all like, 'Holy crap, I can fly, you guys!' He's become something new, and so have you.

Up to this point, your identity is largely shaped by your parent or carer, but your brain is very much affected by puberty too and you'll develop a much keener sense of who you are. EVERYONE is undergoing this rapid change and influx of brain chemicals called hormones. Even the insouciant lions are going to feel like very square pegs being squished into round holes.

Go easy on your grown-ups. This is a tough time for them too.

1. You getting old means they are definitely getting old.

2. They miss the cute baby version of you.

3. You might have very different ideas about your future.

Mum: 'I really think you should stick with the football team.'

You: 'I JUST WANT TO WRITE MY EFFING HAIKUS. LEAVE ME ALONE.'

JUST REMEMBER: BEING COOL STARTS WITH LIKING YOURSELF, NO MATTER WHAT CHANGES YOU'RE DEALT.

I'M COOL, YOU'RE COOL

The worst and inevitable part of a social hierarchy is the rule that allows people to get ahead by climbing on top of others. This is called 'vertical climbing'.

If our zoo was stacked this way, the insouciant lions would be on top, the tragic voles at the bottom and the stick insects tucked away where no one could see them. Upward mobility is possible, of course. As we grow up, things change. No one is stuck. But how do you change your cool status? Not by willy-waggling, obviously.

Here's an idea then: you could publically target someone with the same status as you. You could then humiliate him, you could spill water on his crotch to make everyone think he peed himself – TIMELESS! HILARIOUS! Or you could put him down to show everyone how cool you are. By comparison you will automatically level up. You can go up the whole ladder this way. Terrorise and trample others at every rung of the ladder until you've passed them by.

Hopefully you recognise this is NOT a great idea. This is prime SHITWEASEL behaviour. Sadly, shitweasels exist at every stage of the social ladder. Hard to like and hard to respect, it's nonetheless a strategy which works. If shitweaseling works somewhere it will spread like wildfire.

> **Note to shitweasels: If you trample people to get to the top, they will be only too pleased to kick you all the way back down.**

This is why bullying is inevitable and depressing. If everyone is trying to get ahead by using insults and attacks, on any given day a boy will be both bully and victim in his quest to get to the top.

Being truly cool is about being secure with yourself and being secure with those around you. If you're happy being you, you don't feel the need to put others down anyway.

It is a quick fix to pick on someone's appearance, gender, background or sexual orientation. You might get a quick laugh, but you will not gain cool. Remember: The lions are cool because they are cool with everyone else. Nothing fazes them.

SO HOW DO YOU BECOME COOLER?

CONFIDENCE

Not the confidence to sign up to be Danny in a terrible stage version of *Grease*, or the confidence to jump off a bridge on a springy rope over a crocodile-filled river. It's the confidence that YOU ARE ALREADY COOL. This sounds like utter shite, but just by being yourself and owning it, you are already cool.

You are full of Nerve, Uniqueness, Talent and Skill (or NUTS), you just might not realise it yet. You've probably spent most of your school career trying to hide them. Well, no more! Good at tap-dancing? Get on a table and wow people. Know everything there is to know about *Doctor Who?* Wear that scarf with pride. If you are confident at being you, then nothing anyone does or says can really dent the surface. The daft thing is, it really is that simple. You don't need to willy-waggle, you just need big NUTS.

A DEBBIE-DOWNER

If you're feeling fragile, perhaps leave this section for another time. (I'm sorry, but I'm going to get all Serious Sally for the next few minutes.) We've accepted that shitweasels and baboons are inevitable, but what if it's worse than a bit of banter?

The tricky thing with bullying is recognising it. I don't think anyone wakes up and thinks, 'oh I'm going to do some bullying today', but we get caught up in what feels like a joke. Well, it's not very funny if the joke's on you. If you're honest, I bet you've been guilty of this at some point. We all have.

If a person is repeatedly singled out for ridicule, either in real life or online, it is bullying and it needs to be dealt with. It's too serious not to be. Every year young men just like you kill themselves because they feel they cannot cope with bullying. It's those pesky hormones again. They are likely to make you feel up, down, vulnerable, invincible and even aggressive, all of which can make you behave in ways you might not have before.

What if you're on the receiving end?

1. Write every incident down somewhere. This is evidence, keeps dates straight in your head and is a visual way of showing people how bad the situation has got.

2. Find a teacher or adult you trust and show them your evidence. Seeing it in black and white is always shocking and enables you to show you are being repeatedly targeted.

3. Very often 'bullies' don't recognise their shitweasel behaviour so seeing all of that in print will be very hard for them to wriggle out of.

4. There are numbers and websites at the end of this book that will help you access much more info on bullying.

PEER PRESSURE

This is not a mysterious compulsion to go hang out on a pier. Unless, that is, you have a friend getting all up in your face saying 'go hang out on the pier, all the cool kids are doing it ...' in which case you are a victim of pier peer pressure.

Peer pressure is when people in your social circle or age range (your 'peers') try to get you to do stuff you may not want to do. If it's happening frequently this is a type of bullying. We often don't realise it, because, as well-meaning as they may be, this sort of pressure often comes from friends.

The obvious stuff associated with peer pressure is alcohol, drugs and cigarettes. If your mates ARE partaking you might feel a silent pressure to join in even if they AREN'T circling you, waving fags around, saying, 'Go on, Dave, just try it, you'll be loads sexier if you do,' like in a bad teen soap. You think your mates are cool, so doing what they do will make you cool too, right? Not necessarily.

A couple of things: you have to be eighteen to buy cigarettes and alcohol and (unless they are prescription medications) most drugs are illegal. Doing illegal stuff isn't the way forward cos you'll go to jail (and what you heard about showers in jail is true).

Moreover being really drunk and smelling like an ashtray is NEVER sexy. I don't know why campaigns go on about health problems, I'd be much more worried about sexy people gagging and running away when they get a whiff of a walking brewery with yellow nicotine-stained teeth. AND, since the smoking ban, smokers have to lurk, Gollum-style, outside pubs and restaurants in the drizzle like social lepers.

BUT YEAH, WHILE WE'RE ON THE SUBJECT, SMOKING AND EXCESSIVE DRINKING WILL MAKE YOU THAT LITTLE BIT MORE DEAD EVERY TIME YOU DO SO.

Back to peer pressure. You really have to draw on your inner lion for this one. If your friends are doing something it's SO HARD to refuse – but are you a cloned sheep? It's that timeless pearl your gran (if you have one) probably spouted: 'If your mates jumped off a cliff would you?' Answer: 'Probably ...'

I'd like to be mature about this. If you are compelled to try something, you think it's safe (and legal) and you're surrounded by people you trust in a familiar place, then this isn't the WORST thing that could happen. (Just remember that NO illegal drug is 100% safe.)

If you have a horrid feeling that something is WRONG and you do NOT want to join in with whatever behaviour is freaking you out, call on your inner lion and simply say, '**not for me mate thanks**,' or, '**I'm OK, ta,**' or, '**nah you have it mate, I'm good,**' or, '**I'll just watch,**' or the ever popular, '**I'll watch the bags and coats**'.

I PROMISE in 99 per cent of situations where something like that has happened to me, my chums have been DELIGHTED as it simply meant MORE FOR THEM! In the 1 per cent where people will persist and badger you to do something you don't want to do, walk away – that sort of person is a shitweasel.

Think about it. Why do they want you to try something so badly? I'd argue it's to alleviate their guilt at doing something wrong by sharing the responsibility out. They want to normalise something they know isn't right, or they simply want to see you make a fool of yourself. Bottom line is, going along with something just because everyone else is doing it like a cloned sheep isn't especially cool at all.

THE STUFF TRAP

A common misconception amongst young men is that cool stems from THINGS. The notion that the right trainers, the right watch, the right gadgets will get you noticed has existed since an influential caveman rocked leopard skin instead of lion and declared he was dabomb. Lesser cavemen followed and became the first fashion victims.

But it's not really 'stuff' that makes you cool. It's about conformity versus individuality. Puberty is the time when many of you will stop being a generic 'little boy', who 'just LOVES football, burgers and dinosaurs', and become an individual.

But how much should you show it? When climbing the social ladder it is probably easier to fit in, but this approach will only ever qualify you to cloned sheep status. Being a sheep is on one hand very safe, but on the other very dull. Sheepery is a sure sign that you're lacking in confidence.

Individuality requires big NUTS. It's about saying, 'I like my purple hat, so I'm gonna wear it!' Shitweasels will be the first to target your purple hat because taking the piss out of anything that makes anyone different in order to climb the social ladder is, you guessed it, prime shitweasel behaviour. It's up to you to decide if you have the NUTS to tell the shitweasels where they can stick your purple hat (Answer: UP THEIR GREASY ARSES).

You have to decide if you want to be cool or if you want to coast? Nothing is less cool than being decked out head-to-toe in designer labels and heavy branding. Looking like a bargain bin version of Kanye West is a sure sign of a tragic vole desperately trying to fit in with the cool kids. It's very try-hard. By definition insouciant lions do not need to try very hard.

Like what you like, wear what you like. Be the one to set the trends, not follow them.

SEXYCOOL

It's not a big surprise that women and men alike are attracted to cool. It's not really the cool, it's the confidence.

Think about it. Jabbering baboons are embarrassing. Peacocks are stupid. Shitweasels are evil. Cloned sheep are worriers. Hugely visible eagles are ambition-led. All these species will get mates, but it's the lions suitors really want.

For a start, the confidence and inner security will show in conversation. No one is less impressed with willy-wagglers than potential lovers.

One girl I asked about this topic said,

'All that flashy shit is really see-through. Money and presents and stuff. Why can't men just talk to us like we're human?'

Look at girls as your mates. They are not an alien species, so talk to them like you would a guy. We're all the same, remember? A great and interesting conversation is much more likely to impress than 'flashy shit' and willy-waggling.

More than anything, a guy who is at one with himself and his environment is very appealing. Who wants to date an angry person? No one! If a guy has loads of issues with himself, his body, his hair, his friends, with his family, with the world at large, he is likely to be no fun AT ALL. Who wants to shag that guy? Answer: NO ONE.

CHAPTER 3

LOOKING GOOD

LOOKING GOOD

How many times have you heard someone say:

'It's what's inside that counts.'

LIAR

Let's face it, the bit on the outside counts, too. Why? Because unless by the time you read this book:

a. we've developed telepathic powers
b. Apple® develop 'iTelepathy'

you're not going to be able to judge with any real certainty what someone's character is like on first glance.

As depressing as it sounds, most people will form a first impression about you within the first ten seconds of meeting you. They'll probably decide if they want to have sex with you in the first two. Sometimes you can convince yourself you fancy someone after some time has passed but, let's be honest – if a relationship is going to work you NEED to fancy them in a red-hot 'I-must-have-you-now' sort of way.

The good news is, BEAUTIFUL BUT AWFUL PEOPLE soon show their true colours. You have to have something to back up the goods or people very quickly lose interest. It's like playing with those dummy handsets in mobile phone stores – they look great but they don't do anything.

Bottom line is this: What's inside IS far more vital than what's on the outside, but the pretty shell is important, too.

THE BASICS

YOU MIGHT SMELL.

Way harsh, but did you know that we are unable to smell our own body odour, or B.O. a lot of the time? A terrifying thought, which means I probably smell, too.

B.O. is caused by bacteria that breed in our sweat. It's totally harmless but OH LORD, WHAT IS THAT SMELL? DID SOMETHING CRAWL UNDER YOUR ARMPIT AND DIE? You see my point. Puberty is when this can become particularly grim. It's just one of those things you'll have to accept.

Remember BATH-TIME? Your mum would fill the tub with Matey's Sailor bubble bath and rinse you from a little jug while you wiped bubbles out of your eyes with a flannel? That was lovely, wasn't it?

WELL YOU'RE TOO OLD FOR THAT NOW, YOU PERVERT.

I'm sorry, but it doesn't matter how early the school bus comes, how late you want to stay up at night on the computer or whatever, you HAVE to shower or bathe EVERY DAY or you will smell and people will make fun of you.

FACT: You should willingly submit to a cleanliness regime because people will then not be repulsed by your stench.

As reluctant as I am to tell you how to wash, we mustn't take anything for granted. In short, wash everywhere with extra attention on the three Ps – pits, penis and poo-hole. Job's a good 'un. If you are one of the foreskin-having majority, get right under there and clean the inside bit, too.

Oh and clean your feet really well. Always ensure they are DRY – this will make foot odour less likely.

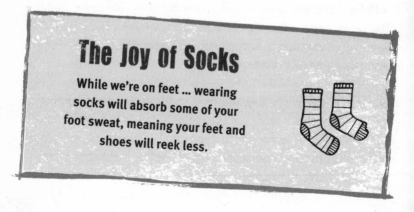

The Joy of Socks

While we're on feet ... wearing socks will absorb some of your foot sweat, meaning your feet and shoes will reek less.

FACE FACTS

The human face is special. We have a whole different part of our brains just to recognise and differentiate them. The face is pretty much the first thing we notice about someone else, no matter how much you may claim to be a 'breast' or 'leg' man.

So how can we maximise our facial appeal? It's tricky, because your face is your face. My advice is this: accept what it is like now. The sooner the better. Your face is in the process of changing, so just go with it. You can't hold back the rain, you can't change what your face looks like. It's worth remembering it's the wonky bits that people find interesting.

Here are some tips on how to make the best of what nature gave you to maximise your pulling potential:

1. TEETH: Never ever, ever underestimate the power of a smile. In the UK, people under sixteen are entitled to free dental care – USE IT. If you have to wear braces or retainers, get it over with while everyone else is in the same awkward stage, too.

Brush and floss twice a day. There is an odd satisfaction to flossing out a really big bit of food, don't you think? I dare you to sniff it, too – it's RANK. Use mouthwash too if you can. Bad breath is one of those things that can stick to someone's reputation like chewing gum on your shoe. Don't let it happen to you.

2. SKIN: During puberty your poor little body, all a-dither, may start to overproduce oil called sebum (everyone makes this – it keeps your skin soft), which can block your skin's pores. These blocked pores can become infected, leading to a zit.

Everyone is going to get spots. I have one right now. But what if it's more serious than that? We're not just talking a few spots here, we're talking about a serious condition called acne. Your doctor will be super-sensitive about this and current thinking is, 'let's sort it young', so they will be able to help.

You don't have to spend a fortune on skin products, you just need to keep your skin clean as you can. The best advice is to wash your face twice a day using a gentle cleansing soap. There, that was easy wasn't it?

> As tempting as it is – don't squeeze zits or blackheads! I know, I LOVE popping a really ripe one, but 'health advisors' frown on it because it can cause scarring and further outbreaks by spreading the pus around. Nice.

Having spots, blackheads or acne has NOTHING to do with how much chocolate you eat or how clean you are. Spots are caused by bacteria called Propionibacterium acnes.

Over-washing, scrubbing, exfoliating and moisturising aren't great for oily, spot-prone skin so step away from the hydrochloric acid and sandpaper.

3. TO BEARD OR NOT TO BEARD: When I was at school, beards were the sole property of Geography teachers and dirty old men. But times change, and sometimes beards and stubble are way hot. However this doesn't mean facial hair is right for everyone.

figure c

Growing a decent beard is actually dependent on having shaved for a few years first to cultivate proper beard hair. Otherwise you end up with what I call a 'hick beard' – sad, downy whiskers, not unlike newborn hamster fur.

Unless you can grow a decent beard, (see figure c). I'd give it a miss.

HOW TO WET SHAVE:

1. Shave after a bath or shower as this makes irritation less likely. Failing that, soak your face with warm water.

2. You need only shave if there's something to shave off. Cover the hairy area, or 'hairea', with shaving foam or gel.

3. Using a clean, new razor blade gently but firmly shave in the direction the hair grows in. Going against the growth will cause stubble rash.

4. When finished, rinse and check you haven't missed bits. Be extra careful shaving around the lips, jawline, spots and moles.

5. Don't shave patterns. You'll look like a dick.

6. Always use some sort of shaving balm as this makes stubble rash less likely.

7. Never apply aftershave straight away, unless you like feeling as if your face is on fire.

Electric shavers are also a great starter tool as you're much less likely to cut yourself.

The age at which you need to start shaving totally varies according to how hairy you are. Everyone is different, everything is normal. For some young men, it could be as young as eleven, but you might not need to start until you're much older.

FAT V. SKINNY

How many hours do you think are lost to people worrying about their weight? I expect it's a number no human could comprehend. If we weren't all so worried about our weight I think we'd have invented time machines and cured cancer by now.

Everyone worries about their weight. Even super-super ripped buff muscle guys are constantly watching what they eat – in fact, they're the worst because they understand alien concepts like 'muscle mass' and 'fat percentages'. It's a general rule that everyone in the world will at any given time think they're too fat or too thin.

Which would you rather have? The good news or the bad news? You can pick which you read first.

THE BAD NEWS: If you want an insanely good body with a six-pack and big muscles you will have to WORK. The ONLY WAY you can have a body like that is through daily exercise and a top-notch diet. No one is born with a body like that. If they tell you they don't work out they are LYING. If you want an excellent body you cannot sit on the sofa five nights a week eating sweets, cake and chips.

THE GOOD NEWS: Working out and exercising is really good for you and fun. Yeah, you have to find the energy and work out what kind of exercise you like, but there's something for everyone. With regular exercise you'll see results pretty quickly AND exercise has a positive impact on your mental health too. A healthy, balanced diet will make you FEEL better also.

MORE GOOD NEWS: People will still want to shag you however big or small you are! (They don't tell you that at school do they?)

MORE BAD NEWS: Problems come when people are unhealthy. By that I mean people who are very underweight or very overweight. Malnourishment is not sexy and neither is morbid obesity. It's because we're programmed to find healthy sexual partners. Forget people wanting to have sex with you though, this is more important – it's about being healthy for yourself. I am not an expert on nutrition or eating disorders, but there are lots of them out there and they will help you if you ask. Check out page 185 for more information.

> It's not rocket science. Eat the right stuff, move about loads.

PEACOCKING

Remember earlier we talked about the peacocks in the human zoo, the gorgeous show-offs? There's a little bit of peacock in all of us, and why not? There's nothing wrong with wanting to look good. However, there is nothing more boring than really, really hot guys who talk about nothing other than the gym and protein shakes. Nothing is less sexy than vanity.

'Tabloid culture' has changed how we view men's bodies. Until about a decade ago, we rarely saw semi-naked male bodies in the mainstream media. As we became hungrier for celeb flesh, actors, singers and sportsmen increasingly became models too.

Celebs may start off quite normal, even though they are famous, but then something strange happens. They start getting ad deals and posing in their underpants. These guys always have smooth, hairless bodies; deep, golden tans; dyed hair; sparkling white teeth.

Gradually the bodies of these guys have become the blueprint that all men want to adhere to.

This is obviously a generalisation. At any given time there are numerous style and body icons to look to, but invariably many sportsmen, film actors, musicians and models have been plucked, waxed, sprayed and dyed in exactly the same way.

The last twenty or so years have seen an exponential growth of the 'male beauty' industry and now men, after many years of sexist imbalance, can also understand the stress of chasing the impossible road-runner of physical perfection.

As mere mortals we have to choose: Do we want to look fake or like an actual human?

BODY HAIR: You'd be hard pressed to find a chest hair on an actor and yet men grow hair there. It even sprouts out of your nipples.

If you don't want body hair, you'll have to pay someone to wax it all off, which is painful, or shave it, but note that chest stubble is as sexy as it sounds. The much-maligned hairy back is also a reality for most men. Let's do some PR on back hair. Instead of 'back hair', let's call it a 'glossy coat' or 'man-fur'. The media shouldn't be allowed to get away with feeding you lies every single day, but I'm afraid they do.

We now have a double-double standard. For years sexist male pigs criticised women for having hairy legs or armpits. These days, they still do, but it works both ways. Sexist female pigs now react in horror to back and bum hair. (Yes, most men have somewhat hairy bums, too.) Why don't we all just chill out and accept that we evolved from monkeys?

PUBES: You don't have to trim your pubes, but I encourage you to do it. A little pubic topiary will help keep everything down there a bit cleaner and it will make your dick look bigger – not that size really matters.

TANNING: Much as with your face and your body hair I need you go to a mirror and find peace with the colour of your skin. All skin colours are cool whether it's 'alabaster white' or 'mocha' or 'deep mahogany' – cheesy authors use these terms all the time because they're ALL good.

HERE ARE SOME TRUTHS:

• Fake tan smells of biscuits and looks well, fake. And you will look orange and patchy.

• Real or sunbed tanning increases your risk of skin cancer massively.

I don't really know how I can make that clearer.

The most important thing I think I can teach you in this book is this: Unless you have a serious monobrow situation, NEVER, ever pluck your own eyebrows unless you want to look like a startled, off-duty drag queen. If you DO, all power to you, my fabulous friend.

TATTOOS AND PIERCINGS: I am covered in tattoos, so don't want to sound like a hypocrite. Like hairstyles and clothes, certain types of body art go in and out of fashion.

Unlike hair styles and clothes tattoos are permanent, unless you want to undergo expensive, potentially painful surgery later to have them removed. In 1999 a 'tribal band' was the height of cool, but by 2009 everyone was getting them covered up with 'sleeve' tattoos. You guessed it, they too fast became EVERYWHERE and I'm afraid a colourful tattooed sleeve can be remedied only by amputation (or painful and expensive laser removals).

With body art I would suggest UNIQUENESS over absolutely anything else. If you're serious about getting a tattoo, choose carefully. Who wants to be stuck with a Sporty-Spice-style Chinese lettering tattoo on their back just because the Spice Girls were 'in' once upon a time? (And I should know – guess whose back it's etched on? Sigh.)

Piercings, like tattoos, come in and out of fashion and the trendy bit to get pierced changes rapidly. Unlike tattoos, piercings can be removed and in time, the scars will heal.

Do be wary however, when contemplating both tattoos and piercings, that even now many employers will be put off by visible body modification. Although daft and judgemental, some people have preconceived ideas of people with excessive body art. You have to find the balance between expression and life-hindrance.

SHOUTING AT CLOUDS:

You can change your hair and you can change your outfit three times a day, but, much like your face, there are some things you are just stuck with. Learning to love yourself *sniggers* takes YEARS, but eventually you sort of stop caring. Remember that there is nothing more uniformly boring than men who spend all their lives looking in the mirror. You have to find the happy medium between making yourself look good and accepting your saggy bits.

YOU CAN DO NOTHING ABOUT THE FOLLOWING THINGS:

- Your height

- Your weight, within reason. (Some of us are naturally slimmer than others, regardless of what we eat. Yep, the old 'metabolism' chestnut.)

- Your skin colour

- Your eye colour (Coloured contacts are weird and creepy.)

- Your shoe size

- Your penis size

Yes it blows, but that's the way it is. Take solace in the fact that EVERYONE IN THE WORLD has bits of their bodies that they hate, especially the gym bunnies – why do you think they hit the gym so hard? Basically it's a worldwide party of self-loathing and you're invited! Grab a drink and a cocktail sausage and let's all be in it together!

A final thought from CLEVER PSYCHOLOGISTS. You might notice that you have a wonky nose or whatever, but other people view you as a WHOLE rather than component parts, which is how we see ourselves. Therefore your wonky nose has little impact on a partner finding you attractive.

Myth Busting:

- All that mad crap that lands in your junk e-mail folder offering pills, potions, creams, spells and enchantments to make your knob bigger are a total waste of time. They are trying to mug you.

- Tugging on your schlong for three hours a day will do NOTHING to increase its size. Also, you can't do your homework one-handed.

- There is NO truth in rumours that height, hand-span or foot size are in any way linked to penis size, which is great because you can't change any of those things anyway.

- There are SLIGHT variations in average penis size of different ethnic groups. Suggesting so publicly could well earn you a black eye.

'ROID RAGE

Beware genies in bottles and men with magic wands. Injecting steroids or growth hormones to bulk up like some inflated, life-size action figure has SERIOUS side effects. For one, your testicles will SHRIVEL UP AND DIE and you'll also be at risk of depression and heart and liver disease. For God's sake, just DON'T.

NIP/TUCK

It would be pointless to deny we live in an unequal society. For some of us, we don't have to make do with the body we've been given because we can pay doctors to change it. This is 'plastic' or 'cosmetic' surgery.

Now while doctors can make bits bigger or smaller, shiny adverts in glossy magazines don't show you the scars, the agonising surgical procedures, astronomical cost or lengthy recovery periods. There's no such thing as a quick fix.

Furthermore, surgery can be a slippery slope. Look at pictures of celebrities who've gone too far. You know who I mean. They look like lumpy pieces of elastic stretched over a Mr Potato Head®. Personally, I think any surgical procedure that's purely for the sake of vanity rather than a legitimate, medical reason is far riskier than learning to love what you already have.

CLOTHES MAKETH THE MAN

I f you haven't skipped this section based on its title, well done, because clothes are more important than you might think.

1. Partners don't want a fashion disaster on their arm let alone their genitals. Shallow but true.

2. I believe clothes are linked to your self-esteem. Wearing drab 'manoflage' advertises a lack of confidence in yourself. Like you don't want to be noticed. The only reason you wouldn't want to be noticed is that you don't feel worth noticing. And that's just bollocks. Let's address that.

As fun as it might be, I cannot individually come shopping with all of you. However, there are a few basic rules that should see you looking hot-to-trot.

Always wear clothes that fit: Whatever your size, wearing clothes that are too big or too small will only highlight your body in all the wrong ways. And really only you know what size the tag says, so it doesn't really matter now, does it?

Do not blindly follow trends: Far, far more important than fashion is fit. Wearing spray-on skinny jeans might well be 'rockstar', but if you don't have the body for it, you could look like a HUMAN MADE OUT OF SAUSAGES. Why would you do that to yourself? Work out your proportions.

CREATE A CAPSULE WARDROBE:

Instead of being concerned about which label you're wearing, I'd advocate buying a series of stylish essentials that you can mix and match over and over.

YOU WILL NEED:

- Two or three pairs of jeans. Jeans are ALWAYS in fashion. ALWAYS. Avoid jeans 'of the moment' i.e. with trendy embellishments, as these date FAST.

- Dozens of plain cotton round neck t-shirts

- Cotton shirts (patterned and plain)

- Knee length shorts (denim or otherwise)

- Wool or wool-mix jumpers: V-Neck and round neck

- A smart outfit/suit in case someone gets married/dies

- One pair of smart shoes

- One pair of casual shoes

- Lightweight summer jacket

- Smart winter coat

- Undies, obviously

There. How easy is that?

That doesn't look like a lot, but with those things you can make about a hundred looks. The fun part is LAYERING. So you start with your jeans and t-shirt. Put a shirt over the t-shirt. BAM! If you're carrying a little weight around your middle there are now parallel lines cutting through your thickest section. If you're slender, do the same but leave the buttons undone to your chest to make you look broader. WOO!

Fashion really is about creating illusion – drawing attention away from your dodgy bits and focusing on your best bits. Above all, wear what you like and what suits you.

But be warned: A well-dressed, confident you is likely to make you attractive to equally foxy onlookers.

THE PENULTIMATE WORD

Why is it that teenage boys' bedrooms so often become gas chambers? People shouldn't be able to smell you before they see you. GO EASY ON FRAGRANCE. That said, don't forget the deodorant. It's all about the balance. No one will want to snog you if you smell like bum OR like you've been attacked by a cologne- wielding shop assistant in a department store.

THE FINAL WORD

There is a word that we don't teach you at school: FETISH. In this world there are people who go for big noses, jug ears, pot bellies, big bums, flat chests, scars, bald heads, back hair and third nipples. So whatever you look like, someone out there is frantically masturbating to pictures of someone who looks just like you. There's someone for everyone, so stop worrying so much!

CHAPTER 4

PUBES AND SEX STUFF

PUBES AND SEX STUFF

Now we've talked about how you're going to FEEL about puberty, let's get cracking with the science part. This is the bit, by and large, that schools do quite well, but frankly some of you will have been taught this better than others.

Puberty can hit at any time from about nine years old in early-starters to as late as sixteen for late-bloomers. Waiting for the changes to start is like waiting at home for a delivery – no matter how many times you ring the company hotline, they refuse to give you any indication of when the goods might rock up at your front door.

Once the first boy in your class hits the 'Big P' it becomes an agonising waiting game during which time a demon voice will grow increasingly loud in your head suggesting that you might be the first biological freak in history to NEVER undergo puberty and therefore be trapped in a state of eternal childishness.

PANIC NOT. Puberty WILL come and make a right old mess of your body. In fact, when it does arrive, although initially filled with relief, you might wish it never had.

Puberty is notoriously unfair. Some boys will effortlessly glide from boy to man, while others are doomed to a phase best referred to as

'Ron Weasley'. The good news is, that whatever it is, no one especially enjoys change. Take comfort that everyone is going through a change even if you all look different.

Also bear in mind that ALL adult humans, male and female, have been through puberty. They mostly survived and if they didn't the cause of death wasn't puberty.

I have found that funny-looking teenagers often become great looking men. A lot of the best looking guys in my school were fat and bald by the time they hit twenty-five while the fugly kids were starting to blossom. Being hot in school is no guarantee of being hot later in life.

What you look like as a teenager has very little bearing on what you will look like as an adult. If you don't believe me, take a cheeky look at page 192.

> This is the thing with puberty:
> You never know what you're going to get.

The difficult thing is you have to do puberty when you are at school, surrounded by lots of other people who are also going through puberty and this can be MISERABLE.

FACT:

According to data from recent surveys, MOST bullying is centred around physical appearance. How shady is that?

THINK:

Before you open your spiteful mouth to make fun of what someone else looks like, just remember: tomorrow you could wake up with a body you hardly recognise. You're all in this together, buddy.

BODY PARTS

In this section, let's look at which parts of your body are likely to undergo remodelling over your teen years.

STARTING AT THE TOP ...

BRAIN: We already mentioned that hormones affect your body in the last section, but this is HOW. They're actually quite complicated. They are chemicals released by various glands that tell the rest of the cells in your body how to behave. These chemicals affect your brain just as much as any other organ, meaning your thoughts and behaviours are going to be MENTAL as you hit puberty. That's because an enormous amount of these chemicals are required to kick-start the change.

The adults in your life will eye-roll and refer to 'mood swings' because they have completely forgotten what it's like to feel inspired and excited one second and then want to drown yourself in acid the next. It's very individual and don't let anyone tell you how you should feel. Just go with it. It's probably just regular hormonal shifts that are a normal part of puberty. But if you think it might be more serious, get help from a trusted adult or doctor, see page 185.

At the same time, your body is getting you ready for having kids, so your brain might start having sexthoughts. WHOA THERE – you're probably thinking – KIDS? I'M STILL A MERE CHILD MYSELF. Correct, but in the olden days you were dead by thirty so you'd have had kids pretty much now, it's just that our bodies haven't caught up to modern living. But you might start having these sexthoughts because your brain is being told to reproduce. So, you are programmed to think about sex. It's totally normal. You might start noticing girls, you might start noticing boys and be even more confused – remember EITHER, or both, are awesome.

FACE: Your face will get bigger, and some features such as your nose and ears may change a little, too. You'll still look like you, just older. See pages 42 and 43 for more on how to deal with zits and facial hair.

VOICE: Over time it will get deeper. Sadly, for many, the teen years are spent in a bizarre REMIX of ups and downs like Will.i.am gone mad on his vocoder. Sometimes it's a dramatic overnight change, but more often than not you'll realise at some point that your voice has become a little deeper.

SHOULDERS AND CHEST: The shoulders, back and chest expand. Your armpits will get hairy. An amount of hair will also grow on your chest despite what topless pictures of famous stars will have you believe. The amount of hair varies greatly between men.

Let's also discuss the dreaded MOOBS or 'manboobs'. During puberty you may gain weight and your chest is likely to expand. Like women, men's chests come in lots of different shapes and sizes. Tell you what, press-ups are amazing for toning the pectoral muscles. As ever, though, if you are concerned with any part of your body, seek the advice of your doctor but remember everything happening to your body is 100% natural.

BACK: Some men also get hairy backs. Perfectly natural, just never seen on waxed male models.

TORSO, OR THE MIDDLE BIT: Most boys will put on a little weight. Just one of those things – usually the weight is distributed evenly so you hardly tell. It's worth noting though, that a lot of research suggests puberty is the time when a lot of young people become highly INACTIVE when, in fact, you need to keep fit more than ever.

GENITALS: Here's the fun part. The penis and testicles will get bigger – sometimes noticeably, sometimes subtly. The change is pretty gradual. Hair will begin to grow over the scrotum or 'ball-sack' and around the penis. This is perhaps the most obvious and potentially alarming change. From an evolutionary perspective we grow pubic hair to alert potential mates to the fact we are of reproductive age. YOU DEFINITELY SHOULDN'T drop your pants in front of girls though. It would be VERY forward.

Back to the 'dropping of the balls'. I hate to burst the bubble, but your balls actually 'dropped' or, more accurately, descended from your lower abdomen just after you were born. This new 'dropping' actually refers to your balls getting bigger and hanging lower. As with all aspects of puberty, this change could be so subtle you might not even notice it happening.

BUM: This will also probably get hairy – mainly in the crack.

LEGS: Hairy. Seeing the pattern yet? MEN HAVE HAIRY BODIES. Although, some don't have as much hair (men of some ethnic origins tend to be naturally less hairy). We all have body hair.

6'6"

6'0"

5'6"

5'0"

4'6"

4'0"

HEIGHT: You'll get taller, obviously. Short men hate being short, tall men hate being tall. Some women like tall men, some women like short men. Don't sweat it, you can't do anything about it anyway. Height is a very geographical thing too. The average height of a man in 2010 was 5ft9 in the UK, but 5ft5 in India and 6ft in Denmark.

So there you have it. Your body is about to, or already has, done some awesome changing. It's a magnificent metamorphosis. I bet caterpillars don't sweat changing into butterflies and we should not worry about changing into men. It's inevitable. It's just that the process (much like a newly hatched butterfly covered in goo) isn't always pretty. The good news is, you have the rest of your life to get used to your new body, and in a few years your childhood appearance will be forgotten lest for hideous and embarrassing school photos.

IT'S GOING TO BE FINE.

YOU AND YOUR PENIS

One of the best things about being a boy is your penis. A girl does not have a penis. The penis is the bit that dangles at the top of your legs above your testicles. It is responsible for waste disposal of urine and, more importantly, sex. Hopefully none of that information is news. If it was, man, we have some catching up to do. Here is a very scientific looking picture:

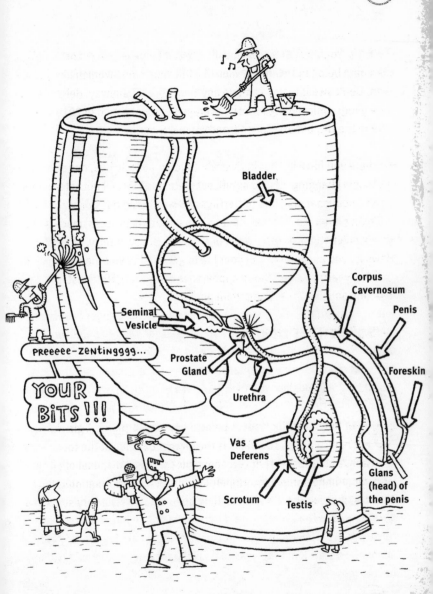

Thank God we can't see all that stuff. It's like a horror film in there. Thankfully, we can see only the good stuff: the penis and testicles.

> **Also, 'Vas Deferens' sounds like a sinister James Bond villain, the sort to have a revolving chair and a white cat in his lap!**

It is healthy from a very young age to see your penis as your best friend. You're going to be together for a long time so you might as well get along. This might sound insane, but a lot of male anxiety is attached to this vital attachment. As mental as it sounds, many men have an angry, combative relationship with their tool: 'Why won't you work? Why aren't you bigger? I HATE YOU!' Don't deny it, you've worried about your penis, right? Fear not. Literally every man has at some stage.

The most famous pervert never to be struck off the medical council was Dr Sigmund Freud. He believed that at about age three we go through something called the phallic stage. He believed this was when boys and girls recognise their bodies are different, and more importantly, that these bits DO STUFF and FEEL NICE. He probably had a point. He said some other stuff too, but it was to do with fancying your mum, so it's best to move on.

The fact that your penis DOES STUFF and FEELS NICE will define your relationship with it for most of your adult life. Therefore it is important that you are totally comfortable with this vital piece of your anatomy – in both physical and mental terms.

First of all, let's decide on names. Genitals, both male and female, are subject to an array of nicknames, some cute, some offensive, some plain wrong. It's parents' fault. Not many parents would refer to a baby's penis as a 'penis', so the identity crisis starts at birth. Let's save time. For the rest of the book, I'LL call it a penis (or sometimes a dick or a cock for LOLs). See page 182 for some seriously awful synonyms.

That's all before we've even mentioned testicles. Let's save some time and call them balls. Anything else is wrong, I assure you.

SIZE: The size of a man's penis seems to be the epicentre of male insecurity. No other body part inspires such concern. Never have I heard a man fret about his stubby fingers or bony feet. As far as I know, no man has ever approached a plastic surgeon to cure his short neck or wrinkly elbows.

The thing that seems to haunt men the most is penis size. Worse still, we can't talk about it. Least of all with other men. This is a real shame. If men were more willing to discuss their penises, a lot of worry could be resolved in about two minutes flat, as men universally realised they are all pretty much the same.

Where does this insecurity stem from? I believe the blame can be laid at the door of one word: MANHOOD. We equate penis size with manhood, as if your knob was an avatar for every inch of your being.

The theory follows that 'the bigger your penis, the bigger the man.' This rubbish is supported by pornography and in our culture, I'm sad to say, bigger is better. We strive for big houses, big cars, big bank accounts. It follows that we should be led to believe a big penis is better than a small one.

I have good news, my friends. This is balls (the metaphorical kind). For many years, the average penis size was thought to be 6.5 inches erect. However, as this was taken from self-measurement, we can be sure the facts were a little skewed because MOST MEN FIB ABOUT PENIS SIZE. More recent data indicates that the actual average penis size is a slightly more modest 5.9 inches erect.

Although Europe 'went metric' in 1989, willies will always be measured imperically. Strange, because having a 14.9cm cock (5.9 inches) sounds quite impressive.

FOR THE RECORD,
THIS IS HOW BIG 5.9 INCHES IS:

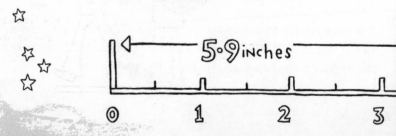

5.9 inches

0   1   2   3

This data presents an average, so of course there will be dicks out there that are considerably larger or smaller – and before you start comparing, remember yours is probably still growing. It's tempting to do some sneaky comparing in changing rooms. It's not a gay thing, it's reassurance. You'll find that some are bigger than others, but it's worth noting that a knob's soft or 'flaccid' state is no indicator of how big it will be when hard, or 'erect'. We call this 'growers' versus 'showers'. A great big soft schlong is literally no use to anyone – remember it's only when erect it can do its sex job. Some penises experience upward of 100 per cent size increase when they go from soft to hard, while others increase only by approximately 50–75 per cent.

This brings us nicely to my next point. Women don't seem overly concerned about penis size. I asked a female focus group (see page 80) 'does size matter?' The overwhelming consensus was no: 'For 90 per cent of men, no. However there is that 5 per cent who are too small/ thin and 5 per cent who are too big/wide.'

NOT PARTICULARLY BOTHERED

4   5   6   7

Interesting. For the first time we encounter a whole new level of fear and paranoia. So you're pretty sure your dick's not miniscule? Well, hang on a second mister! Maybe it's TOO BIG! You can't win. What we're dealing with there are the EXTREME cases. But remember, what doesn't work for one sexual partner will work for another.

We will talk about sex in depth soon, but let's state right at the beginning, sex is NOT all about your penis – if it is you're doing it wrong. Therefore, any worries you have regarding penis size and sex should be separated. However, if you are worried you might fall into the 5 per cent of men who are 'too small', don't worry. Remember what we said last chapter – you might not have finished growing yet, but if you are losing sleep, see your GP or GUM clinic (see page 185) where a professional can reassure you.

APPEARANCE: The simple fact of the matter is that no two penises look the same. Some are thick, some are thin, some have dark patches of skin, some have foreskins, some do not. If we're being really honest, they all look RIDICULOUS. The human body design team were having a laugh that day.

Erect penises rarely poke out from the body at a 90 degree angle. Most have a slight curve somewhere and this can be in any direction. This is totes normal and only a really extreme bend would affect your sex life, for instance a condition called Peyronie's Disease in which scar tissue can cause severe bends. This can still be treated by a doctor.

Whether a penis is cut – 'circumcised', or uncut was much debated amongst the research group. In the UK, less than 20 per cent of all men are cut, with much of this number down to cultural or religious reasons. In the US and Canada, this figure is much higher, with 56 per cent of all US baby boys being cut before they leave hospital. In the US, most parents opt for circumcision simply so their baby boys 'fit in' with the majority.

Since time began doctors have been squabbling about the health benefits of circumcision, although if there are any they are minor. The NHS in Britain will NOT carry out 'elective' circumcisions without medical or cultural grounds. In truth it makes very little difference to you as a boy. The foreskin is very sensitive, so it is another thing that FEELS NICE. (Don't try to chop it off at home.) The foreskin should not be too tight around the head, or 'glans' of the penis. It should be able to be stretched back fully over the glans. If you cannot do this, it might be worth a trip to your GP or GUM clinic. The state of your penis is of MUCH more importance to the women I interviewed. Repeat after me:

AN UNCLEAN PEEN MUST NEVER BE SEEN.

That's right. Your partner – male or female – will not care what it looks like as long as they cannot smell it. You may well cringe, but how clean is your peen right now? This is especially important for uncut guys. You really must get under that foreskin. SERIOUSLY.

FUNCTION: So at this point, perhaps much more important than what your penis looks like is 'is it doing its job?' This is the root of more stress, I'm afraid. This is why we must get away from this idea of 'manhood' being all about your knob.

What does semen look like?

Cum, as it's better known, is a gloopy, white-grey goo that shoots out of your penis. It's warm and sticky when it comes out, but soon dries into a charming, flaky crust.

The best comparison is that weird cornflower gunk you use to thicken gravy or glaze cakes.

(DO NOT GLAZE CAKES WITH YOUR SPUNK.)

Cartoons of white tadpoles have probably really confused you. Sperm cells DO look like tadpoles, but only many, many times magnified.

A standard 'emission' will give approximately a dessert spoon of cum.

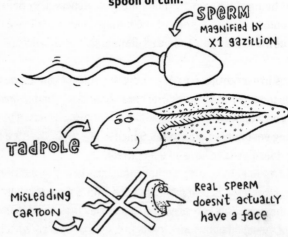

SPERM
magnified by
x1 gazillion

TADPOLE

MISLEADING
CARTOON

Real sperm
doesn't actually
have a face

Your testicles will start producing sperm cells and semen, the gunk they hang out in. And from then on, the rest of your time on Earth, previously dedicated to keeping your parents and teachers happy, is about to get a helluva lot more complicated as you continually fight off the desire to put your penis inside things.

Semen MAY start to find its way out through WET DREAMS or 'nocturnal emission'. This is when your subconsciously stimulated penis has a happy in the night and releases an amount of semen. Not everyone has wet dreams and you don't actually have to be dreaming about sex to get one. In a US study 13 per cent of boys said their first ejaculation was a wet dream. It is thought masturbation is one way of minimising the chances of it occurring, see page 77.

Wet dreams are a cause of much tension as many boys fear the 'evidence' being discovered by their parent or grown up. Hopefully, you'll be able to discuss it honestly with them. If not, don't sweat it because now you know that having wet dreams is totally normal.

Sometimes like any other part of a body, the penis might not do what it is supposed to. With so much pressure about size, shape, smell, name, it's no wonder the poor little fella might get nervous. If you're channelling your entire being into 5.9 inches of your body, it's a miracle the thing doesn't shrivel up and die entirely.

'Erectile dysfunction', 'premature ejaculation' and 'delayed ejaculation' are the three most common sexual problems that men experience. In more fun terms, these mean: 'floppy cock'; 'cums in a second' and 'my wrist is tired'.

Your penis goes hard when blood flows into the soft tissue. It's hydraulics. Sometimes, however, this doesn't happen. There are about a million reasons why – stress, nerves, alcohol, cigarettes, for example and that's only a glimpse. Lots of men under 40 – 10 per cent in fact – will suffer erectile dysfunction at some stage. For men over 40, this percentage increases. This number is a reported figure, so it's actually probably much more common because men don't like admitting it's happening to them out of pride. Remember, if it sometimes happens, that doesn't mean it will always happen.

Obviously, the more you freak out the less likely you will be to get a stiffy. Stop. Relax. Try again in five. Later, you'll see there are a host of things you can do for your partner that don't involve your cock.

Ejaculation is a similar beast. The more you worry, the bigger a problem it will be. Premature ejaculation is common in young men, hardly surprising given that your penis will be so thrilled to be invited to the sex party – you can hardly blame him for arriving a bit too soon. The good news is, this gets better with practice and, in extreme cases, can be treated. Delayed ejaculation is less common, tends to be related to stress and is more usual in older men.

NIFTY TIP: To slow down ejaculation, use a thick or extra-thick condom to reduce sensitivity.

KNOW YOUR BODY:

The fact touching yourself up feels awesome is not the only reason you should do so. In fact, this fun activity could save your life. You should get into the habit of examining your balls for lumps and bumps. They should feel smoothish and roughly spherical. Regular testicular exams can catch nasty diseases like testicular cancer nice and early.

THE ART OF THE CRAFTY WANK

Now that you know all about your penis and how it works, let's have a proper chat about wanking, or 'masturbation' if we're going to get all hysterical about it. You probably know this already, but masturbation is briskly rubbing your penis up and down, usually until you cum, or 'ejaculate'. This is one of those things that FEELS NICE.

Pretty much everyone masturbates. Men and women, who do not have a penis, obviously, but can stimulate their clitoris and the surrounding area. It is COMPLETELY normal – don't let anyone tell you otherwise. Loads of people masturbate and I'm guessing those who say they don't are fibbing. Although be aware that some faiths and religions have different attitudes to it – and that's fine. To each their own!

It is quite hard to have a wank when you're a teenager. This is sad, because it's the time in your life when you'll want to do little else. Experiencing your first wank is like finding an unlimited-refill pot of gold under your bed. Your body can do this amazing thing, as many times as you like, and it's FREE!

It's tricky though. You probably share a home with a minimum of one parent, or at the very least an adult. Throw in siblings and the horror of shared bedrooms and bathrooms. There's an ancient proverb: 'The family that wanks together, goes to jail together'. So that's unacceptable.

Lack of privacy makes it almost impossible to take ten minutes to pleasure yourself. Fear not, one day you'll be in charge of your own laundry and you can mess up those sheets every day if you wish, but until then here are some top tips for wanking subterfuge!

1. Wipe clean surfaces – Easy cum, easy go

2. The shower wank – Self-cleaning

3. The 'I-need-a-poo wank' – People won't even go in the bathroom after you're done and there's already loo-roll there.

4. The crusty sock – Lives under your bed and slips into any washing machine unnoticed.

5. Get it on yourself – You are much easier to clean than bedding and you won't have to lie in a sticky mess all night, unless you like that sort of thing …

MYTH BUSTING

This almost goes without saying: Masturbation is a normal, healthy part of being a human. If it wasn't, it wouldn't FEEL NICE. There is no truth to claims that masturbation is in any way harmful to your health.

HOW OFTEN IS NORMAL?

By now, you have hopefully realised that 'normal' is a word that should be taken out and shot at dawn. When it comes to having a cheeky wank, your 'normal' will be different to the guy (or girl for that matter) next to you on the bus. DON'T STARE AT HIM!

I recall breaking into my sister's bedroom (sorry!) to steal her issue of *More Magazine* as the problem page featured a young lady writing in to ask if her boyfriend was ADDICTED TO MASTURBATION because he wanked twice a day. Needless to say, this article raised more questions than it answered.

Let's be sensible. Wanking is free and healthy. Your body is physically capable of cumming again mere minutes after you've shot your wad (although this varies from dude to dude). I mean, if you're at it like ten times a day, I'd be concerned about chaffing, but it's probably not going to kill you. I refuse to put a number on what is normal. On a busy day at school followed by a trip to kung-fu and then Pizza Express, I can't imagine you'll have much time to beat one out. On a rainy January Sunday when the TV is broken, I can think of little else you'd want to do.

That said, a bit of 'self-love' is a delightful bonus of human reproduction, not a way of life. Go ride a bike or read a book, too.

MANHOOD

A final word on you and your penis. In all three cases, size, appearance and function, we need to get away from the idea of your penis being YOU. It is only one part of the whole you. Your manhood is about so much more than your 'manhood'. Comforting words from the focus group:

> [The penis] doesn't rate all that highly for me. I'm much more likely to focus on a man's body, face, eyes and so on.

As it is wrong to objectify women, it is also wrong for them to objectify your penis – if a partner is hung up on a part of your body, I'd argue they aren't worth knowing.

Remember, your penis is the last thing a partner is likely to see so why spend all that time worrying? By the time a partner sees your penis, they will already like you just for being you.

STOP EVERYTHING

Before you go any further, you have to decide if you're ready for this. This chapter deals with the ins-and-outs of sexy time.

It's not sexy, it's not saucy, but it's honest, warts and all.

The problem is this. Once you know these facts, you can't unknow them. You may spend the rest of your life having sex, so if you don't want to know this stuff just yet, then skip this whole chapter and continue the important business of being young and pure as the driven snow.

THE PROBLEM WITH PORN

*O*pening scene: A pretty girl, dressed in a cheerleader uniform, makes *her way down a quiet suburban street. Evening is drawing in, the light fading. Pigtails swinging, she looks up and down the street. She is wary.*

In the shadows, a steely, silver car prowls, its engine low. The girl, Mel, continues her walk, keeping her eyes fixed firmly on the pavement. She's alone on the darkening street.

The car crawls closer. Black eyes watch her, reflected in the rear-view mirror. Mel's eyes widen Her heart beats faster as she becomes aware of the vehicle. Why is that car moving so slowly? Is the driver lost?

The cars pulls into the next junction, blocking Mel's path. The passenger window slides open with a hiss ...

Mel is trapped.

Scary stuff huh? It might surprise you to learn that this is not, in fact, the opening scene of a teen slasher film in which a sinister driver cruises the streets looking for defenceless cheerleaders, but is actually the opening scene to a porn film. The sinister man proceeds to lure Mel into his car with the offer of a lift home. He then takes her to his home, with its hideous 'rainforest' wallpaper. They then do lots of different types of sex with Mel, who is clearly in her early thirties, spouting sex talk in a cutesy, baby voice.

You can find porn like that and more online in about ten seconds. The Internet has changed sex education forever. Aged about eleven, you're taught how babies are made and how babies are born, but you're not told how to deal with seeing web pages full of X-rated images. By the time you get to the end of primary school, it's entirely possible you've already seen things that would make your poor teacher weep.

VISUAL AIDS

Since time began, men and women have used visual aids to complement masturbation. There's a reason all those stick figures in cave paintings are nude, dear reader. (Go ahead, palaeontologists, prove I'm wrong!)

You should be grateful. Before the advent of the Internet, we had to make do with underwear models in home shopping catalogues or join porn-sharing syndicates whereby well-used magazines were hidden in exchange spots in the local woodland. These things still work today of course, but the Internet has cut out a lot of barriers to pornography access.

Theoretically, anything that gets you going could be classed as porn. For most people, sexual fantasy begins with a TV star, film actor or musician. The mere idea of having sex with a celebrity or someone in real life – how mundane – is often enough to get a person off.

The pornography we need to discuss is the HARDCORE STUFF. We're talking actual people having actual sex in films and photos. If you've managed to avoid this stuff, I'm glad you've emerged from the rock you've been living under long enough to find this book.

I believe pornography roughly falls into the following genres, although they do sometimes combine a selection of them:

SOLOS: Individual porn actors pleasure themselves. Element of danger provided by terrifyingly long fingernails in close proximity to clitoris.

GIRL-ON-GIRL: Self-explanatory. Some men just don't like seeing a male porn actor's penis. Also, remember what I said about society thinking this is sexy and cool.

DUOS: In most heterosexual porn the scene features a man and a woman engaging in lots of things that FEEL NICE.

GROUPS: Two men and a woman; two women and a man; two women, two men; $3x=y-12$. The possibilities are endless.

NO PLOT: Much porn goes like this: the pair enter a room, with resigned, robotic precision. Following some deeply awkward chat, they get on with it – very often you can see subtle clock-watching. There is no story, but there may be character roles e.g. gardener, schoolgirl, pterodactyl. (This last one exists. Seriously.)

PLOT: Sometimes however, there will be a plot. These porn stars engage in dialogue before the inevitable sex happens.

FETISH: A tricky category, since anything that gets anyone going is strictly a fetish. Broadly speaking though, this is the 'kinky' stuff that involves specialist gear and kit. Sometimes, you may mistakenly believe you've clicked onto a horror film.

Now, some reactionary types would tell you that PORN IS BAD. IF YOU WATCH PORN YOU MIGHT AS WELL PAY SATAN UPFRONT FOR YOUR TICKET TO HELL. I believe this is an unhelpful approach to take in a world where pornography is unavoidable. More to the point the above claims are inaccurate. Still, we are dealing with a secretive, sometimes murky, and many would argue, exploitative, industry.

It is very difficult to know if what you are watching is morally sound. There is no way of knowing if the people you see in porn are happy and healthy – a lot of porn actors LOVE their work and good on 'em. Selecting pornography made by the big LA studios is perhaps safer than low-budget home-video style ones where a sad, glassy eyed couple do it in a mildew-covered bathtub next to crusty bottles of cheap shampoo.

With this in mind, let's move on to the problem with porn.

OK, HERE GOES ...

Putting aside the moral implications of watching porn – you can't be expected to change the world from your bedroom, least of all when one of your hands is busy – we must think about the direct consequences of getting sex education from pornography.

Let's say it together: **PORN IS NOT SEX EDUCATION.**

I assume you've seen at least one Batman or Superman film? Yes? Following this film did you leap off a building in an attempt to fly? No? I hope not. If that did happen, I'm really sorry for bringing it up.

This is the real problem with porn. As sex education in schools doesn't dare go the places that pornography does, young men like you are left with a gaping void in their knowledge. We tell you how the baby gets there, but not the actual 'doing it' part.

This book is aiming to fill your void. *snigger*

Think about porn actors. They are professionals. No one is expecting you to be a professional. Just like you shouldn't perform open heart surgery after watching *Casualty*, you shouldn't attempt sex the way you've seen it in porn or read about in certain bestselling erotic novels.

PORN, LIKE BATMAN, IS PURE FANTASY.

1. **It is a film.** They are shot with multiple camera angles to provide flattering images, using multiple takes to get it right.

2. **The actors are selected on the basis of looks and talent.** If we believe porn, women do not have pubic hair. Hell, most of the men do not have pubic hair. The majority of actors are exceptionally gym-fit, giving a skewed image of what a naked body looks like. They have fake tans and, ready for this, bleached bottoms. Many of the female actors have breast implants. The male actors have much larger-than-average penises.

3. **The actors have done this many times.** They are not nervous or even horny. They are feeling nothing. It is a job. As such, they are very experienced and can do 'advanced moves' that beginners cannot.

4. **The situations are fiction.** Most day-to-day scenarios do NOT end in sex. The pizza delivery man just wants to give you the pizza, get a respectable tip and piss off.

5. **No one is wearing a condom** or talking about sexually transmitted infections, or 'STIs'.

6. **In reality, when men or women say 'no' during sex, this means STOP.** In porn-land, characters sometimes keep going, which is rape.

Again, except for the last two, none of these things are BAD or EVIL. One may enjoy porn in the same way one may have enjoyed Batman. It's escapism.

The problem comes when guys try to recreate porn. Again, you are not the pros. The women I spoke to UNANIMOUSLY agreed that they could tell if a male partner had been exposed to porn. The warning signs? Excessive moaning; expectation that a woman will cum at the mere presence of a man in the room; 'jack-rabbit' or 'smash the doors down' sex.

Here's the thing. A 2010 study found that while 70 per cent of men admitted to watching porn, only 30 per cent of women did. There could be some fibbing going on but let's assume that more men than women watch porn. This is hardly surprising. Nearly all porn is made for men by men. The sad fact is that porn usually caters to the sexist notion that women are there to provide men with pleasure, not the other way around.

So we cannot blame girls for being less than impressed if boys turn up expecting the full porn-star treatment. Unless you happen to be dating a porn-star, this is unlikely to happen and even then she might want a night off.

Now, I'm making generalisations. It is entirely possible your partner might be into hardcore, moany, groany, PVC-clad sex. Some women are. Some men are.

THIS IS THE BIT THAT NEITHER SCHOOLS NOR PORN IS TEACHING YOU: YOU HAVE TO TALK ABOUT SEX WITH YOUR PARTNER.

Yes, as scary as it might sound if you think you are ready to have sex, then you should be mature enough to talk about it. ASK your partner what FEELS NICE. They will definitely know. Some of those ideas you've got from porn? ASK if your partner likes the sound of them. Speed it up or slow it down? For God's sake ASK!

In truth, your partner will be thrilled at this level of respect. You have taken their feelings and sexual desires into account. Admitting you don't automatically know what pleases someone is honest and honesty is very sexy. The whispered phrase 'what do you like?' is one of the most important you will ever learn. These conversations might be a little bit awkward at first. I'll tell you what's more awkward though – the bit where you wee on your partner because you saw it in a porno one time and your partner cries. THAT will haunt you forever.

Sex is best when it's 'real'. Real sex has unflattering light, flat hair, unsightly bulges, leg cramps and squelching noises. It has laughter, red faces and bodily fluids.

PORN MAY BE MANY THINGS, BUT IT IS NOT 'REAL'.

THE SEXTING GENERATION

Since the advent of the camera phone, everyone became an overnight porn-star. No one is immune: pop-stars; premiership footballers; reality TV stars. It has almost become expected that illicit pictures and/or videos will be swapped as part of the human mating ritual.

Technology has made it too easy. That said, we ALL have to accept that doing this is monumentally stupid. We are doing something risky AND leaving evidence that can spread round to others faster than chlamydia.

TAKE THE SEXTING QUIZ:

1. Which of the following is illegal?

a. A hot 16-year-old taking nudey pics of their body

b. A hot 16-year-old putting nudey pics of their body on the web

c. A hot 16-year-old sharing nudey pics of their body around

Answer: ALL OF 'EM! That's right. The age of consent might be 16 but ANY erotic image of a person under 18 is classed as an 'indecent image of a child'.

2. Which of these is also illegal?

a. You taking risky pics of your super hot 16-year-old partner

b. You uploading risky pics of your super hot 16-year-old partner to the web

c. You showing your friends risky pics of your 16-year-old partner

Answer: You guessed it – all of 'em again. Same story: 'indecent image of a child'.

3. And last but not least, which of these come with a jail sentence?

a. Looking at nudey pics of 16-year-olds on the web

b. Looking at nudey pics of people who 'appear to be under 18' on the web

c. Accepting nudey text pics from a 16-year-old partner

Answer: Absolutely no prizes for guessing ALL THREE. This is classed as making and possessing CHILD PORNOGRAPHY.

> Think really, really hard the next time you consider sending someone a picture of your bits. One day you might want to be a politician. A family doctor. A squeaky-clean TV presenter. You probably won't be able to do these things if everyone's seen your junk all over the Internet or you've been arrested for looking at, sharing, making or possessing child porn.

Last and perhaps most importantly of all, even if the pictures you are taking and uploading are of yourself, you are still distributing indecent images of a child.

So you see, even if 'everyone is doing it' this is a really dodgy area, especially for young people such as yourself. Please don't do it.

BAN THIS SICK FILTH

YOU, SEX AND THE LAW

In the UK the age of consent, or age at which you are legally allowed to have sexyfuntime is 16, regardless of your sexual orientation – whether you like boys or girls. However even if you ARE 16, you can't have sex with someone over the age of 18 if they are in a position of trust, like your teacher or doctor or something. Got that?

This kinda goes without saying, but sex with ANYONE under 16 is a) wrong and b) a crime. Even if you are over 16 and some superhot 15-year-old is well up for it and you do the deed, this is known as 'statutory rape' and it could see you in trouble.

Why bother with consent laws when we know there are people younger than 16 doing all the sex? They protect you. Yes, YOU. It is a fact of life that lots of people, young or old, but especially young, don't necessarily know what's good for them. Most six-year-olds, given the choice, would opt for daily meals of candyfloss sandwiches, for example. This would NOT be good for them. It's the same with choices regarding your sex life. People vastly cleverer than I have set those laws at 16 as this is the age at which they feel you are finally able to make mature(ish) decisions about sex. Anything less than that ... well, the theory is 'you might THINK you know what you're doing, but let's give it a few years to be sure'.

Even once you are 16, before you have sex, it is important to make sure everyone wants to do it or this is what is called rape. In recent years there have been some high-profile court cases where young men have found themselves in court because a sexual partner has alleged that they never consented to sex, sometimes because they were too drunk or semi-conscious. If your partner, whether they are a girl or a guy, is unable to give consent then this is also rape.

Rape is not just penetrative sex of a vagina or anus either. Oral or digital (hand) sex would also count.

It's dead easy really: Just make sure you ASK before you do the sex. If she/he says 'yes', you're off, if she/he says 'no', it's off. Even if your partner changes their mind halfway through the sex, you MUST stop. If she/he does say no, don't push it. Go home and have a wank.

DOING SEX

Even though your body is more than capable of doing it, you might not be ready emotionally. Sex IS a big deal, especially when you're young. Don't let anyone tell you otherwise. Peer pressure is bollocks. As soon as early rumours of people in your class or circle of friends 'doing it' start to spread like wildfire, there can be a real pressure for everyone to start 'losing it', and by 'it' we mean 'virginity'. This pressure to ditch your v-card as if it were cursed isn't very sexy to you or prospective partners.

Similarly, if all this sex malarkey just isn't all that appealing, or if the thought of someone else's genitals plain terrifies you, this is another sure sign that now isn't the time for you to be doing the sex. This is also fine. I always think you'll KNOW when the time is right for you. A natural curiosity seems to blossom in us all at some point, but like everything relating to puberty, the day it arrives in your head and heart will be totally different to your next-door neighbour.

But what if you really want to have sex but can't? Welcome to real life, mate! Pressuring and harassing partners to have sex is about as sexy as the smell you get when you leave a bit of raw chicken in the bin on a hot day. No one likes a slathering, horny teenage boy humping their leg like a dog in heat.

IF YOU'RE HORNY, DO EVERYONE A FAVOUR AND HAVE A WANK. YOUR TIME, MY FRIEND, WILL COME.

A piece of wisdom: if every loud-mouthed shitweasel was REALLY having as much sex as they brag about, do you really think they'd be wasting time CHATTING ABOUT IT? No, they'd be off DOING IT. I find the more people brag about sex, the more imaginary it is.

Anyway, you'll know when you want to have sex because you'll really, really want to. So when the time comes and remember the time will come, how do you do it and how do you do it well?

The good news is, you have your whole life to practice getting good at doing sex. No one is expecting you to be a first time porn star, THANK GOD. Remember what a turn-off that can be!

Instead, I want you to remember this: LOADS OF THINGS FEEL NICE. If you do lots of these things (not all at once), and remember to ask 'does that feel nice?', your partner will think that you are the best sex-doer there has ever been.

Here are the basics – the areas that feel nice.
There's more than you think!

All the same bits feel nice on YOUR body too – with two small differences.
First, and one would hope obviously, you have a penis which is insanely
sensitive and you also have a prostate gland up your bum which feels nice
when stimulated. So whether you're into boys or girls, you should be
targeting roughly the same areas.

Vagina:

Confused? It's not your fault, you don't have one and yet you're
expected to be an expert. Here's the basics. Wee comes out of the
'urethral opening'. You don't put your willy in that bit. You put your willy
in the vagina. It's easy – it's the biggest, most obvious hole.

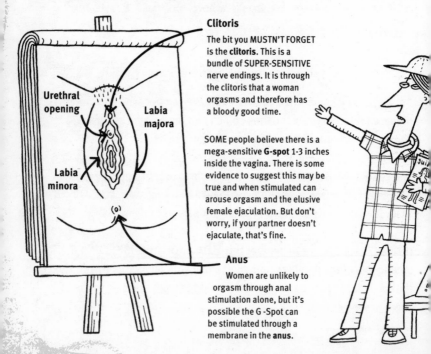

Clitoris

The bit you MUSTN'T FORGET
is the **clitoris**. This is a
bundle of SUPER-SENSITIVE
nerve endings. It is through
the clitoris that a woman
orgasms and therefore has
a bloody good time.

SOME people believe there is a
mega-sensitive **G-spot** 1-3 inches
inside the vagina. There is some
evidence to suggest this may be
true and when stimulated can
arouse orgasm and the elusive
female ejaculation. But don't
worry, if your partner doesn't
ejaculate, that's fine.

Anus

Women are unlikely to
orgasm through anal
stimulation alone, but it's
possible the G-Spot can
be stimulated through a
membrane in the **anus**.

Urethral opening

Labia majora

Labia minora

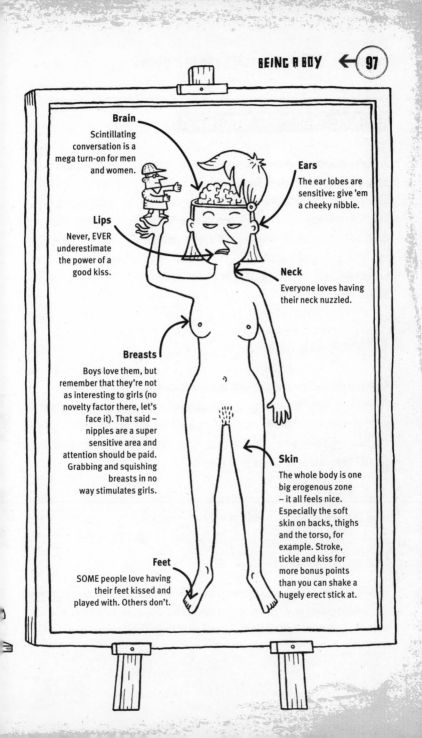

Brain

Scintillating conversation is a mega turn-on for men and women.

Ears

The ear lobes are sensitive: give 'em a cheeky nibble.

Lips

Never, EVER underestimate the power of a good kiss.

Neck

Everyone loves having their neck nuzzled.

Breasts

Boys love them, but remember that they're not as interesting to girls (no novelty factor there, let's face it). That said – nipples are a super sensitive area and attention should be paid. Grabbing and squishing breasts in no way stimulates girls.

Skin

The whole body is one big erogenous zone – it all feels nice. Especially the soft skin on backs, thighs and the torso, for example. Stroke, tickle and kiss for more bonus points than you can shake a hugely erect stick at.

Feet

SOME people love having their feet kissed and played with. Others don't.

A FINAL WORD ON VAGINAS:

We talked about how penises look different, yeah? Well so do vaginas. Just as porn would have us believe all penises are rock-hard and about eleven inches long, it also tells us that all vaginas are tiny, hairless and have internal labia minora. **They all look different, but all are normal**. If you are gonna be funny about what a girl's vagina and surrounding hair looks like, don't be surprised if she laughs at your cock. If body parts are making you squeamish, this is another sign that you are probably not quite ready for a sexual relationship.

FOREPLAY

You have to think about sex. It's not a race to stick your penis in things. Contrary to what you may have heard, there isn't a contest and you won't win anything once you do. Take it nice and slow – you'll get more out of it and so will your partner. Attacking your partner like a sexual ram-raider is unlikely to win you any fans.

Think of it like a super-fancy dinner. Even if the main course was a bit crap, if there was a delicious starter and dessert, you're less likely to mind. That's why, if you do lots of different things which feel nice, your partner is likely to go away happy.

This is where foreplay comes in handy. Never go straight to penetration. The whole point of kissing, stroking and touching is that it turns you both on and readies the body for what's about to happen.

IN WE GO

Having done lots of nice foreplay it's time to get going. Let's break it down into nice, easy parts.

ORAL SEX: Not surprisingly this means 'do it with your mouth' and tongue. The clitoris or penis can be stimulated orally and, yep – you guessed it – it FEELS NICE. Watch the teeth, though, NO ONE likes that. If you ejaculate, or cum, in a girl's mouth, she cannot get pregnant, but there is a risk of sexually transmitted infection, see page 122.

Stimulation of the penis is achieved by moving the mouth and tongue up and down the shaft, allowing pressure to build. The word 'blow-job' is misleading in that no blowing occurs – it's more of a sucking motion. A woman's clitoris and the surrounding area can be licked, sucked and kissed, too.

DIGITAL STIMULATION: Sometimes it's quicker and less messy to just do 'handies'. Remember it's her clit you're looking for, not just the hole. You and your partner can also stimulate each other by rubbing and stroking your penis. Never apologise for lending a hand, either, sometimes you need a hand to cum and sometimes so does your partner. In fact while we're on the subject … Sex doesn't always finish with cumming or an orgasm. It's nice if it does, but if you or your partner don't cum it's not the end of the world and it's nothing to be ashamed of or worried about. This is another porn hangover – in porn everyone ALWAYS cums. In fact, female porn stars often start screaming with pleasure if a man breathes near them. In real life, not so much.

VAGINAL SEX: This is the one you need to do if you want to make a baby. You can't just plug it in like an iPod and expect the magic to happen. The penis must be rubbed in and out until ejaculation. It's the friction that does the trick. Your partner can also achieve orgasm through stimulation of the clitoris and arguably the G-spot. During sex, the vagina cleverly lubricates itself to make sexual intercourse easier for both of you.

Contrary to the sex-ed films you might have seen in school, there are lots of different ways of doing vaginal sex. Standing up, sat down, lying down, on the side, her on top, you on top, you on your head ... You get the picture. TALK ABOUT IT. What position feels best for you? What position feels best for her? **Despite what porn has taught you, pounding away like a steam engine on speed is NOT the way forward.** Start SLOW to allow your partner to get used to the alien appendage currently poking about inside her.

Vaginal sex shouldn't HURT, but it may be uncomfortable the first few times a girl has sex. Be aware of this to make her and your early sexual experiences positive ones, unless of course, you actively enjoy girls referring to you as 'dickhead'. Also, if she doesn't have an orgasm when you're having vaginal sex, that's fine. If that's the case, try some of the other things that feel nice, like oral or digital sex, to help stimulate her instead. It's worth noting that additional lubricant – which you can buy from any chemist – will reduce friction during sex. Just make sure you get a water-based lube as oil based lubes (such as Vaseline) can split condoms.

If any of your spooge ends up in her vagina, or even near her vagina, it is possible you will make a baby. Don't believe ANY old wives tales about certain positions preventing you from getting pregnant. It is even possible for a girl to get pregnant when she has her period. So make sure you wear a condom.

ANAL SEX (AKA BAN THIS SICK FILTH):
Even though there may be brigades of angry Internet people carrying flaming torches, it's important we talk about this however controversial it seems.

You don't have to look very far to find anal sex in porn. I'm talking straight porn here – we'll talk about gay men in a while. There is so much anal sex in straight porn that you'd think it was the most common thing in the world. However, a 2012 US study found only 44 per cent of straight men had anal sex at least once in their lives, while 36 per cent of women reported the same. That's less than half, you guys. It is also worth noting that not all men that have sex with men like anal sex.

Anyway, anal sex is inserting your penis into your partner's butt.

TWO THINGS:
1. Anal sex hurts the bum.
2. If you have anal sex, don't be surprised if you get poo on your winky.

If you want to have anal sex you will need some lubricant, or lube, because the anus does not lubricate itself. You cannot make a baby via anal sex, but as the anal passage is particularly delicate there is a heightened risk of contracting STIs through this type of sex.

In order to minimise the 'poo-on-your-winky' situation, some people prepare by cleaning their anus thoroughly or 'douching' – squirting water into their back passage.

Although I made that sound like quite hard work, a lot of people really enjoy anal sex. There's only one way to find out if your partner does ... ASK!

I'm not sure I said the word anal enough. **SO ANAL.**

SILENCE IS GOLDEN?

Another spanner to throw in the works: What should one say during sex? Silent sex is notoriously creepy. No wants to hear passing traffic at the height of passion, but screaming, 'OOOH YEAH, OH YEAH BABY, JUST LIKE THAT, SAY MY NAME,' belongs firmly in the domain of porn stars and erotic novels.

So what's a boy to do? Encouragement is always good. Let your partner know what they're doing well and they'll do more of it – a positive sexual feedback loop if you will. This can be conveyed with well-timed groaning or a quick 'that's amazing'. If you want to groan, go on, but be aware of the poor neighbours.

> **The dirty talk dilemma: a bit of filthy chat CAN be a turn on, but ONLY if both partners are into it.**

DOING SAME-SEX SEX

Most young people are *fascinated* with the idea of same-sex sex – both men and women. I imagine this is because no one really talks about it because 'it's rude'. (FYI, it's not.)

Here are the basics for two men and two women. Note I didn't say 'gay' – remember you don't have to identify as gay to have sex with someone who is the same gender as you.

MAN ON MAN: Two men can do lots of things that FEEL NICE. Don't forget the ears, lips, neck and so on during foreplay. Oral sex, digital stimulation of both the penis and prostate gland up the bum and anal sex all FEEL NICE.

WOMAN ON WOMAN: Two women can do lots of things that FEEL NICE. Oral sex, digital stimulation of both the clitoris and G-spot and anal sex, stroking the ears, lips, neck and so on. Two women may use sex toys such as vibrators and dildos for penetrative sex.

Common Misconceptions 101

In same-sex relationships one partner is 'the man' and one is 'the woman'. This is nonsense. It's either two men or two women. That's sort of the whole point, duh.

It should be pretty clear that same-sex sex is VERY like mixed-sex sex. There are so many incredibly dumb rumours about same sex couples but a lot of it is our fault, by that I mean grown-ups, TV and school, for not telling you the whole truth. More or less, human beings are like little Lego bricks – we all click together quite neatly – male or female.

Baby Talk

Two men can adopt a child or use a surrogate to have a baby. Two women can also adopt a child, use a surrogate or have a fertilised egg implanted in one partner's uterus in a process called 'in-vitro fertilisation', or IVF, if they want to be parents. But biologically, same-sex partners cannot conceive a child by having sex.

FREQUENTLY ASKED QUESTIONS FROM ACTUAL YOUNG PEOPLE:

WHY DO PEOPLE HAVE SEX IF THEY DON'T WANT BABIES?:

A very common question. The answer is because IT FEELS NICE. You know how eating cake is pleasurable? So is sex. You should probably aim to have sex as much as you eat cake – often, but not so often you make yourself sick.

WHY DO GIRLS USE VIBRATORS?

You know how wanking feels good for boys? Well it also feels good for girls. A vibrator is a battery or mains operated device that feels nice for girls. It is used to stimulate their clitoris and, possibly the G-spot.

HOW LONG SHOULD SEX LAST?:

Cackling hen parties joking, somewhat cruelly, about how 'he didn't last two minutes' may have led to some anxiety about the duration of sexyfuntime. Oh poor Penis, he has so much to worry about. As mentioned before, sex is VERY EXCITING, sometimes you might get over excited and cum quite quickly. It happens.

If you finish first, it's no biggy – focus on finishing your partner.

We already talked about how using a thicker condom will reduce sensitivity, but I don't think guys should be overly worried. The good news is, even if you do cum quickly, after a little rest you can do it all over again.

Like an all-you-can-eat buffet of sex, intercourse should be a delicious mixture of snacks and feasts. Sometimes a three minute, explosive session is megahot, while on other occasions a more considered, lazy afternoon in the sack is called for. This comes back to what we said about foreplay. Actual intercourse shouldn't really last for much more than ten–fifteen minutes TOPS. Everyone would start to chafe and it is quite tiring, y'know. BUT with loads of nice foreplay, the experience will last longer and the cackling hen party will have nothing to taunt.

> **Don't forget the 'after' bit. Cuddles and kisses followed by cups of tea and/or bacon sandwiches will make your partner feel valued.**

HOW TO TAKE OFF A BRA

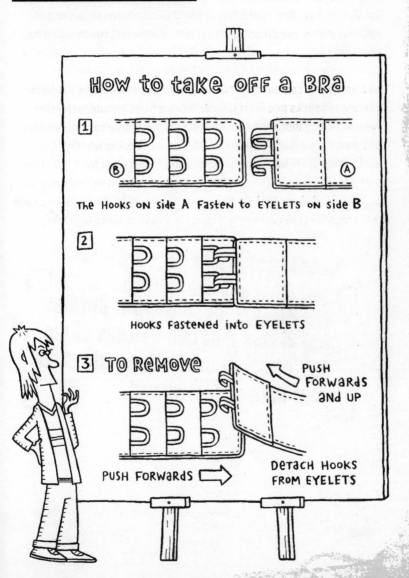

How to take off a BRA

1. The Hooks on side A Fasten to EYELETS on side B

2. HOOKS Fastened into EYELETS

3. TO REMOVE

PUSH FORWARDS and UP

PUSH FORWARDS →

DETACH HOOKS FROM EYELETS

CAN YOU HAVE SEX IF A GIRL IS ON HER PERIOD?

Yes. In this case red signals 'go'. HOWEVER, there are things to consider: If a woman is about to get her period, she may be feeling a bit CRAP. She may have painful headaches and stomach cramps, which can continue throughout her period, so she may not want to have sex. Also, be aware that a woman CAN still get pregnant, even during her period, as the next egg may well have been released. Women are also MORE vulnerable to STIs during this time as the cervix wall is weakened. Sex on a period is also likely to be messy, but then as you will be WEARING A CONDOM that will make it easier to clean up!

'Check your privilege' – we'll never know what it's like to have a period every month, so be extra nice to girls at this time.

WHY DO PEOPLE SCREAM DURING SEX? IS IT HURTING?

Most histrionic screaming during sex is a reflection of a) pleasure and passion or b) amateur dramatics. Sometimes sex does hurt but in sort of a good way – like having a deep tissue shoulder massage.

I hope this section has enlightened you, even if just a little bit. There are more common sexual terms in the glossary. If you still have questions, although it's awkward, I'd ALWAYS recommend talking to a trusted adult over searching on the Internet. **ALWAYS**.

CHAPTER 5

ALWAYS WEAR A CONDOM

ALWAYS WEAR A CONDOM

How much clearer can we make it? This is the WORST THING ABOUT a lot of PORN. No one wears a condom. Oooh it makes me mad because, to anyone watching porn (i.e. YOU), it looks like it's OK. Well it isn't.

GOOD SEX

You know what makes sex really, really good? NOT WORRYING is what makes sex really good. Nothing squeezes the fun out of sex like a) anxiety, b) guilt, c) rashes and d) babies.

If you have unprotected sex, two of these four things (a and b) are inevitable. If you are having sex without a condom you might have made a baby, or caught something and feel guilty because you might have given your partner something. If you aren't feeling these things after unprotected sex then you bloody well should be.

CONSEQUENCES

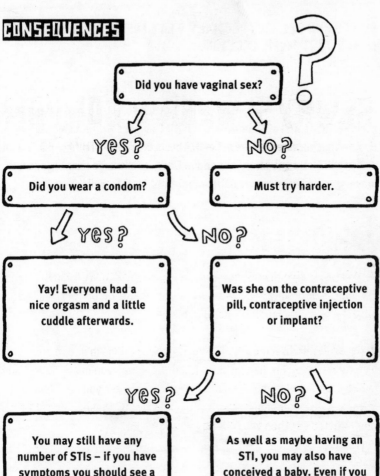

Did you have vaginal sex?

YES?

Did you wear a condom?

NO?

Must try harder.

YES?

Yay! Everyone had a nice orgasm and a little cuddle afterwards.

NO?

Was she on the contraceptive pill, contraceptive injection or implant?

YES?

You may still have any number of STIs – if you have symptoms you should see a GP or go to a sexual health clinic ASAP. Even if you DON'T have symptoms you may still have an STI.

NO?

As well as maybe having an STI, you may also have conceived a baby. Even if you didn't cum inside her, sperm cells are present in pre-cum. Also these methods are NOT 100% reliable.

AS YOU CAN SEE, IT'S PROBABLY A LOT EASIER FOR EVERYONE IF YOU JUST WEAR A CONDOM.

What's more, sexual partners will have god-like levels of worship ready for you if you whip out a condom. Why? Because it's a sign you respect their health as well as your own. GO YOU! This goes without saying, but ensure your condoms are intact and reasonably new – don't keep a condom in your wallet for years and expect it to work. The same goes for keeping them somewhere too hot or too cold such as a car glove box.

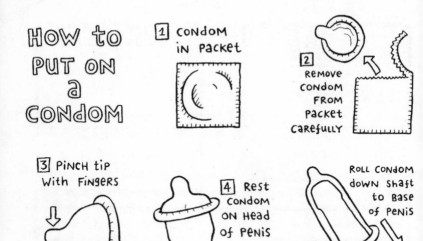

HOW to PUT ON a CONDOM

1. CONDOM IN PACKET

2. REMOVE CONDOM FROM PACKET CAREFULLY

3. PINCH tip With FINGERS

4. REST CONDOM ON HEAD OF PENIS

5. ROLL CONDOM DOWN Shaft to BASE OF PENIS

You can totally practise this at home alone. It's called a FANCY WANK.

You can get an unlimited number of FREE condoms from your GP or from a sexual health clinic, most of which run completely confidential drop-in sessions for young people. Failing that you can buy condoms from any supermarket, garage, pharmacy or pub toilet in the country.

There really isn't an excuse.

Always carry a condom – just in case.

FREQUENTLY ASKED QUESTIONS FROM ACTUAL YOUNG PEOPLE:

CAN CONDOMS BE TOO BIG OR SMALL?

Condoms are usually made of a rubber or latex material, meaning they are naturally skin tight on even the most petite of penises yet can stretch to accommodate even the biggest whopper. This said, those clever manufacturers have seen fit to make them in various sizes for the larger gentleman, not to mention latex-free for those with allergies. Basically, you can't use THOSE excuses not to wear a johnny.

WHAT IF A CONDOM BREAKS?

A cause of much stress, this is exactly what emergency hormonal contraception – formerly known as the 'morning after pill' – was made for: emergencies. It should NOT become a substitute for other methods of birth control such as condoms or contraceptive pills. Emergency hormonal contraception will be effective, but increasingly LESS effective for five days after your condom breaks and is available over the counter from a pharmacy, sometimes for free, or from your GP or GUM clinic. If you are concerned you may have been exposed to HIV, you can speak to your doctor about an emergency treatment called PEP or 'post exposure prophylaxis'.

WHY ARE CONDOMS FLAVOURED?

This oddly eighties gimmick seems largely over now. Making condoms in a wild variety of flavours is to cater to oral sex, while others are ribbed and shaped, allegedly to heighten the pleasure you will receive during sex. I mean, for crying out loud, you're having SEX – how much more pleasure do you want?

It doesn't matter if they have spoilers, subwoofers and alloy wheels – as long as they prevent spooge from entering the looloo, that's all that counts.

IF SHE'S ON THE PILL DO I NEED A CONDOM?

In a word, yes. The combined pill is 99 per cent effective, but do you fancy being the poor 1 per cent that's a father? What's more, the pill is only 99 per cent effective if taken precisely as instructed, so you should remind your partner to take her pill. Upset stomachs and other medications will make the pill less reliable. For example, if your partner has vomited within two hours of taking her pill, she needs to take another. Finally, the pill, contraceptive patches, gels, rings, injections and intrauterine devices, or IUDs, do NOTHING to protect you from sexually transmitted infections, or STIs.

HOW BABIES ARE MADE

I think this stuff is pretty well covered in schools, but just in case there's any confusion, let's clear it up:

The guy makes the sperm and the girl releases one egg a month from her ovaries (which we don't have). The egg hangs out inside yer missus waiting to be fertilised by your sex-wee. If it IS, the little tiny baby thing, called an embryo, latches on to the uterus wall and bingo! You'd better start knitting. If the egg is NOT fertilised the girl will lose the egg and uterus lining once a month as her period, a bloody discharge from her vagina.

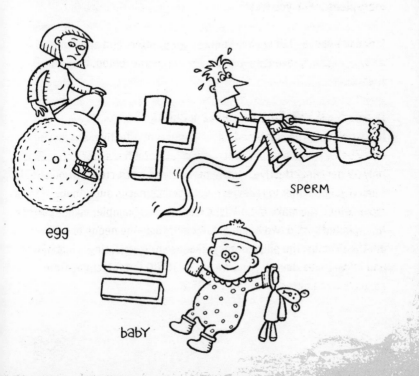

egg

SPERM

baby

DO YOU WANT A BABY?

If you do not use a condom when you have vaginal intercourse you may well make a baby.

Do you want a baby? I don't know, maybe you do. BE SURE, BE VERY SURE. Babies take all your time AND all your money. Being a parent is the most challenging thing human beings do, even if it is mind-blowing and wonderful. Having a baby changes EVERYTHING. Your life will never, ever be the same once you have a kid.

If a woman gets pregnant, or 'conceives', then nine months later she will give birth to a baby. You will be forever responsible for the baby, financially and emotionally, if she decides to keep him or her. Not only will the Child Support Agency hunt you to the ends of the earth for money, but you'll also have a lifelong connection to the little tiny baby and its mum, even if you are not together and don't raise the baby or spend a lot of time in its life. Even if you decide to give the baby up for adoption you will always be emotionally connected to the baby. Just something to be aware of.

There will come a time however when you might REALLY, REALLY want a baby and when that day comes, finding out your partner is pregnant will be the best news ever. Being ready for a family is a little like knowing you're ready for sex – you'll know. You'll be with someone who you think is SO AWESOME you want to semi-replicate them using 50 per cent of your own genetic code. That sounds sci-fi BECAUSE IT IS!

Humans do nothing more amazing than reproduce – do it on your terms when you're ready, not because you couldn't be arsed to use a condom that one time with your cousin's mate on a pile of coats at a party.

THINGS YOU SHOULD KNOW ABOUT ABORTION

Abortion, or a termination, is when an unborn foetus (little squiggly baby thing) is removed from a woman's womb before it could live by itself in the outside world. If this happens by accident, it's usually called a miscarriage, if the procedure is carried out by a doctor it's most often known as abortion.

There are approximately a BILLION reasons why a couple or an individual might choose to have an abortion – sometimes it's just not the right time to be having that baby. Sometimes young people have abortions, sometimes older people have them. People who have already had children have abortions, people who have had abortions go on to have kids too.

However, as with emergency hormonal contraception (the 'morning after pill'), abortion REALLY isn't a replacement for a condom. Why? Because it's not very pleasant for you or your partner.

Firstly, abortion is a faff. In the UK, for an NHS abortion, you have to get two doctors to agree the procedure is in the woman's best interest. A pregnancy in its very early stages can be aborted 'medically' with pills – which may have horrid side effects, while pregnancies up to 24 weeks can be terminated 'surgically' – a process which basically involves a surgeon sucking the foetus out with a pump. I cannot imagine this is fun, and no surgery is without risk. I'll tell you what IS fun: using a condom.

You should also be aware that abortion is a very hot topic. Some people think it is WRONG, some people STRONGLY feel that women should have greater control over their reproductive rights. To avoid dealing with such a thorny subject, just use a condom, OK? Thanks.

If you find yourself needing to talk to someone about abortion, you can speak to your GP, visit a GUM clinic or talk to Brook (contact details can be found at the back of the book).

Douche alert

Emergency contraception and abortion aren't contraception – they're emergency brake levers. There should be a fine for improper use.

Both are unpleasant – more so for women than men, so don't put your partners in that situation unnecessarily.

Accidents happen and that's why emergency hormonal contraception and abortion are important, but they are much harder work than using a condom.

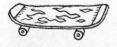

STIs

If you are sexually active, it is possible that at some stage you might well get an STI, or 'sexually transmitted infection'. There's a ludicrous stigma attached to STIs – we wouldn't be shy about saying, 'oh I caught a cold off her', or, 'he's the one I caught chickenpox off', would we? But no, because some infections are passed around by *whispers* SEX, we are very squeamish about them.

That said, no one likes having a poorly peen or miserable muff and perhaps that's why STIs are seen as worse than a cough or a cold.

Should you catch one, and it might not always be obvious, just go to the doctor or sexual health clinic. Most are easily treatable and testing usually involves little more than doing a wee in a cup, so there's no excuse. However, prevention is better than cure so ALWAYS WEAR A CONDOM.

THE ONES YOU CAN SEE:

GENITAL HERPES: Nasty, painful and itchy sores on your penis or anus. Basically a cold sore on your knob. Cannot be cured – you'll carry a dormant version of the virus for life – but can be treated. Once infected, victims may well experience further itchy/painful episodes.

GONORRHOEA, AKA 'THE CLAP': Although not always symptomatic, the most pressing symptom is a burning sensation when you pee, although some sufferers may also get a delightful pus-like discharge from the penis. As it's bacterial it can be treated with antibiotics. Oral gonorrhoea is on the rise too – the bacteria can live on your tonsils following oral sex.

GENITAL WARTS: Genital warts are caused by a virus called HPV which is present in about 30 per cent of all sexually active people. It's highly contagious but, of those, only about 3 per cent will ever develop a wart on the penis, vagina or anus. Visible warts can be treated with wart removal cream, cryotherapy (freezing them off), cutting them off (ouch!) or burning them off with electro- or laser therapy. If those methods weren't unpleasant enough, the virus remains forever and recurrence is possible.

SYPHILIS: Large, non-itchy, non-painful ulcers on the genitals or anus are the first sign of syphilis. This one needs to be treated quickly with antibiotics or there could be secondary symptoms. Syphilis can be fatal if left untreated.

A clever tip:

Peek inside your underwear. If you can see a discharge, this is a sign you could use a visit to a clinic. Similarly look for droppings ... pubic lice leave their poo in the host's pants. Yep! Lice poo!

CRABS: This one is well confusing. WHY would you have crabs DOWN THERE? Turns out 'crabs' is a name for 'pubic lice' – sort of nits for your pubes. You can see them AND they're super itchy. They can be treated with a lotion but they can be a pain to get rid of. As well as the itching, crabs have the embarrassing side effect of you having to 'fess up to your folks because the lice can live on bedding, clothes and towels. Therefore affected items need to be boil-washed, or you could potentially give your mum crabs.

THE ONES YOU CAN'T SEE:

CHLAMYDIA: Well, in about 50 per cent of cases you might experience a slight discharge or a burning sensation when you pee. Or you might have chlamydia and never know because you don't have any symptoms. BUT the consequences for women are much more serious as the bacteria can lead to severe reproductive problems. It's worth noting it can lead to sterility in men, too, so you might not be able to have children. In 2011 approximately 186,000 people were treated for Chlamydia in the UK, making it by far the most common STI. That's just the ones who were treated too.

HIV: HIV (the virus) and AIDS (the response to the virus) are NOT going away. HIV and AIDS do not affect ONLY gay men and drug users. ANYONE can get HIV if they are having unprotected sex with a carrier of the virus. There is NO cure for HIV. Sorry that was all a bit Debbie-downer, but this super-serious disease just isn't talked about in the way it once was. Although on first infection there may be flu-like symptoms, many people carry the virus without knowing it. The only way to be safe is ... as you know WEAR A CONDOM!

HEPATITIS B AND C: There's a whole alphabet of Hepatitis viruses out there, but these are the ones mostly commonly transmitted via sex. It's an infection of the liver and can be very serious. Hepatitis B can be vaccinated against.

This whole section is hugely depressing. I can't tell you how itchy I was while writing it. It's like as soon as someone says HEADLICE you start scratching. While we're being SERIOUS, let's also mention that drinking copious amounts of alcohol and having sex don't go hand in hand. Research shows that young people are much more likely to make POOR CHOICES regarding safe sex while under the influence of drink and drugs. It's also worth noting that having sex while one or both of you is drunk is usually pretty terrible for everyone involved.

CELIBACY

Celibacy means 'having no sex' either through choice, or because you're just too ugly – KIDDING! Celibacy isn't a cool term, but I think we should dust it off and use it more often. I think it's FINE to say, 'I don't want to have sex right now,' or, 'I'm not ready to have sex'. I think this is especially OK for young guys, maybe even you, who might not be ready for it yet. Even if you are ready and have had sex with one partner doesn't mean you have to do it with another. Do you know what's really good? KISSING AND HOLDING HANDS! Seriously! You can get all the same intimacy from a lovely cuddle, so don't be railroaded into sex if you aren't keen.

I think we should talk about TRADITIONAL VALUES for a moment. No, don't run away, it's important! Some people have cultural or religious reasons for being celibate and that's fine, too. However, people with such values often still have sexthoughts and might even WANT SEX. Just because you WANT sex, doesn't mean you have to have it. Lots of people want to wait until they are married or whatever and you should always respect the beliefs and opinions of others, even if they are different to your own.

It's worth mentioning that not having sex is by far the most effective way of not getting pregnant or catching an STI. I know, I know! Just saying ...

So, to wrap up (get it?), unless you're a) in a trusting, committed relationship and really believe your partner is somehow incapable of cheating on you (REALLY?) b) are trying for a baby and c) have both been screened and cleared of STIs, let's say it together:

ALWAYS WEAR A CONDOM

CHAPTER 6

BEING A BOYFRIEND

BEING A BOYFRIEND

DISCLAIMER

This book in no way guarantees you,
'the reader', a shag or even a snog. James Dawson,
'the author', accepts no liability for slaps-in-the-face
and hoots of mocking laughter.

HOW TO PULL

Now you know HOW to do the sex, I suppose it's only fair to give some advice on how to meet people to do the sex with, otherwise it's very much a solo event.

Be honest. Have you ever thought in your darkest hours that you might never meet someone? Or that you might and they won't like you? Everyone has these thoughts. The good news is that there are nearly seven billion people on Earth and those who are post-puberty are nearly all trying to get laid. The odds are ever in your favour.

TV LIED

This is becoming a theme, right? In TV, mating works like this:

1. Boy meets girl in school or workplace.

2. Intial 'hate' relationship develops in to grudging respect.

3. Argument in pouring rain followed by passionate kiss and instant marriage proposal.

Sometimes this, or variations of this, actually happen. You might meet a girl or guy as part of your day-to-day life and you will have a natural reason to chat to them about work or school so there is no need for you to use 'lines'. You fancy them and they fancy you back. That DOES sometimes happen. It happened to at least two married couples I know.

HOWEVER, the rest of us have to be a bit more proactive. You COULD sit around and wait for the beautiful girl/guy to walk into your life, but you might be waiting a really, really long time.

Therefore, the rest of us have to GO DATING or GO ON THE PULL.

DATING

Even if you DO meet someone naturally, you still have to talk to them, so even the lucky few might need a little help. The best place to find out if there's 'something there' is to take someone on a date. Talking to people you fancy can be nerve-wracking because sexthoughts are the natural enemy of logical thinking. Hopefully we can make the process as painless as possible.

Step 1:
The ask and the answer

So you met someone, either in real life or cyberspace. Say to the object of your desire: 'Do you wanna go out sometime?'

Your new love-chum will say 'YES', 'NO' or 'WHO ELSE IS GOING?', which is a polite way of saying 'I don't like you like THAT'. If she, or he, says no, start sending letters made from cut-up magazine letters. Oh no, wait … DON'T do that. Instead move on and take it like a man. You don't fancy everyone in the world, and the rest of the world isn't forced to fancy you.

Step 2:
Choosing a venue

So they said yes? YAY! This next decision is going to depend on your budget. The actual venue of the date isn't important, as long as you have somewhere to chat. Therefore the cinema or theatre aren't actually that great unless you're going to get food before or after. Restaurants are the classic option, but a walk in the park – during the day, idiot, unless you want them to think you're a weirdo – is free and serves the same purpose. Bowling alleys are always good because if you run out of things to say you can chat about the game. NB: Always let your date win.

Step 3:

Conversation

On a GOOD date, conversation will flow naturally because you'll have loads of shared interests. However, a good rule of thumb is BE INTERESTED. Don't throw out facts about yourself and present opinions or you'll look like a self-involved cock. Instead ask questions, find out about their life. Your date will also ask questions which you should answer honestly. This is how you'll find out if you like each other.

Safe topics involve family, school, work, music, TV and hobbies. Stay away from money, politics and religion.

Step 4:

Leave 'em wanting more

This is SO important. Even if you're having the BESTEST TIME EVER AND IMAGINING WHAT YOUR KIDS WILL LOOK LIKE, you should end the date.

Firstly, if a date goes on too long it can run out of steam but more importantly, if things are too intense it can all get a bit scary and off-putting. There's nothing nicer than going away wanting more. If the date has gone well, end it with arranging the second date. If it hasn't gone well, don't promise a second date you have no intention of keeping.

Step 5:

Aftercare

Also vital. The follow up 'I had such a nice evening' text is a great way of making the other person feel great. DON'T do this if you have no intention of making a second date.

If a date didn't go well, a polite, 'I'm not really looking to start anything at present', is far better than stringing her along. If it was a bad date, it's likely they sensed it too – it's not all about you now, is it?

Now this is all very well if you've met someone already, but what if you haven't? How do you meet someone in the first place?

ON THE PULL

In Da Club: There are 'night clubs' where people go to flaunt their sexual wares to prospective partners. Sometimes it's also just to have a dance, but mainly clubs are there to enable single people to meet in an environment where almost everyone is on the pull.

Now, in all honesty a lot of people 'in da club' are just looking to have fun – a cheeky snog or some no-strings attached, or 'NSA' fun. This is fine as long as we're all honest about it. If you do meet someone you like you can always leave them with your number to arrange a later date. Clubbing isn't a contest. If you leave without a snog, you haven't LOST.

If you're having trouble finding someone, how do you go about it the RIGHT way?

THE HUNT: Identify your target – this will be someone you fancy based purely on physical grounds.

THE CHASE: Scope your target. Are they single? With someone? If so, abort mission.

THE KILL: Make eye contact. Is eye contact returned? Lack of eye contact is a SURE SIGN they are not interested. Eye contact held? Smile. Smile returned? Advance.

THE CHAT-UP: Whether you're 'in da club' or not, you may well have to make the first move and open the conversation. For something so impossibly simple, so many of us get this wrong.

My personal favourite is a friend of mine who was approached with the opening gambit: 'You seem like a really cold person.' I mean, REALLY? He thought THAT was going to get him a shag? Another? 'You'd be really fit if you lost the tummy.' I mean PHWOAR, right?

DISCLAIMER

If you think you might like guys and you're not sure if a guy you like ALSO likes guys, this process can be SUPER-tricky. This is why a lot of guys who like guys go to 'da gay club' because most of the guys in there will like other guys. Man, that's a lot of 'guys'.

Actual Bad Chat-Up Lines You Should Never Use

'So ... do you watch telly?'

'Is your surname Jacobs? Because you're a cracker!'

'What growls and shags like a tiger?' *Growls*

'Are you a plumber? Cos when I saw you my nuts tightened.'

A guy who presented his 'card' which was, in fact, his number on a cut up cornflake box.

'What's got two thumbs and a massive cock?' *displays thumbs*

I think some guys struggle when talking to women because they incorrectly believe they're taking to an alien race, thus adopting a strange seduction language they think will impress. FACT: women are humans and speak Earth languages. If we have FRIENDLY conversations as FRIENDS we'll all do a lot better. Remember way back when I said you should talk to girls like they're your guy friends. Well, you should.

START WITH 'HI, HOW ARE YOU?'

Unless she's a horrid and rude person, she'll reply with, 'Fine thank you, you?', or launch into a lengthy diatribe about her ill mother and two-faced best friend, in which case, edge away slowly.

'I'M GOOD, THANKS. I'M ROMEO.'

Again, unless you're dealing with a very impolite person, she'll say: 'Hey, Romeo. I'm Jules.'

Now this is where it gets tricky. You could go for the classic:

'WOULD YOU LIKE A DRINK?'

This works only in places that serve beverages, of course. It gives the mark an obvious jumping on or off point. If she says 'yes', she's vaguely interested, if she says 'no', she's not. Simple as that. So the conversation is open. Now refer back to the section on dating. Ask questions, be interested. If you really have to have a chat-up line, make it complimentary.

Always compliment on non-arbitrary things. For example, saying, 'you have lovely eyes', can be met only with a cringe-face. What's the response to, 'you have lovely eyes', other than a conversation about dominant and recessive alleles? Instead go for something she CHOSE. For instance, 'What an amazing tattoo/piercing/necklace'. This opens the door to a starter conversation about the tattoo artist or a comparison of body parts you have pierced. Also stay well away from generic platitudes such as, 'you look great', or, 'you're beautiful'. Instead focus on something specific. 'You look great – has anyone ever said you look a bit like her from *Twilight*?', or, 'How do you walk in those shoes? That takes skill!' Be aware that any line is only a conversation starter, you'll have to do the rest.

ON THE STREET: Now this is MUCH riskier and you'll need rhino-sized balls to pull it off. The problem with this is that 'in da club', most people are either with their partner or trying to find one. In the queue at the Post Office, most people are just trying to post things (or because they're in purgatory). Other than a wedding or engagement ring, there's no way of telling if someone is single or not. The only thing you can look out for is eye contact.

AT SCHOOL OR AT WORK: Ah, the joy of the captive audience. When you fancy someone at school or work, it's great because you get to see them every day for prime stalking. However, this is also the downside because if the chat-up goes wrong you're stuck with them and THE SHAME.

As you're at school or work with them, you have way more time to figure out if you like them or not, so there's no pressure to 'pull'. My advice would be to let things take their natural course.

THE INTERNET: It's not just kiddie fiddlers who use the web to meet people these days. More and more of us are meeting people this way. Some people use dating sites for dating, some use them for NSA. Again, be honest about your goal up-front.

DO be aware that most dating sites have age limits, usually 18, but that doesn't stop younger teens flirting outrageously on Facebook or Twitter. You MUST follow all those rules your teachers tell you about e-safety: never give out your address online and see the rules about sharing explicit images on page 90. These rules are so simple that even the horniest of us can remember them. If you ALWAYS imagine your online conversations are with a crusty, bearded perv, you'll be a) a lot more cautious and b) delighted when a pretty girl called Sarah actually turns up for your brightly lit, public date.

Not Interested?

What if a potential suitor tries to pull YOU but you're not keen? You don't have to to snog everyone but don't be a turd about it.

Try: 'Tonight I'm just here to celebrate my friend's birthday'; 'I've sort of got my eye on someone else' or just, 'you're not really my type ... sorry'. If you are KIND and HONEST anything is fine. DON'T make prolonged eye contact with people you don't fancy, because it will mislead them.

TEAM HOT VS TEAM FUN

The most important thing to remember when going on the pull is:

BE YOURSELF.

There's no point in pouting, posing and gesturing when meeting new people (in da club or elsewhere). At the end of the day, you want someone to fall for the real you – the one who likes licking the chocolate off a Jaffa Cake while watching cartoons in bed. Pretending to be someone you're not to get someone to like you is a sure way of exhausting yourself. Keeping up an act is really hard work.

Also it's worth remembering that TEAM HOT might look sexy, but they also look unapproachable, vain and stand-offish. TEAM FUN – the guys and gals who are having a great time with their mates – look much more like the guys you'd want to get to know better and they are usually pretty darn good-looking, too.

THE SUBTLE ART OF KISSING

Far, far more than you hear people criticising sex, you hear them evaluating the simple kiss. Kissing is very important as it's a trailer for sex. You know when you see a movie trailer for a film that looks terrible – you're unlikely to pay £11 at the cinema for the full feature film? The same is true of kissing and sex.

Kissing is all about LIPS: **L**ocation, **I**nsertion, **P**ressure and **S**aliva.

LOCATION: You shouldn't be surprised to learn that you should be aiming for your partner's mouth, or more precisely lips. However, what might come as a surprise is how many people fall at this first hurdle. 'Face eating' is a big problem in our society. You expect a partner to kiss your lips and before you know it, your nose, eyelids, ears and chin are covered in drool.

Talking you through a good kiss is difficult. In simple terms you need to part your lips slightly and massage the top or bottom lip of your partner between yours. This sounds hideous, but feels lovely, I promise. The goal is not to dock with your partner's mouth. It's about the lips.

You can gently kiss your partner's neck or earlobes, but I'd suggest anywhere else, facially speaking is a bit weird. Never have I heard anyone say, 'then he kissed my eyebrow and I was in ECSTASY!'

INSERTION: The amount and duration of tongue action varies wildly between individuals. Some people just aren't keen on 'French Kissing', as precisely no one calls it any more. I would suggest that NO ONE wants a big, fat tongue thrust halfway down their throat.

Where is our happy medium? Most kissers enjoy a bit of tongue-touching and it's usually pretty easy to follow your partner's lead on this. If in doubt, GENTLY pop a bit of your tongue into their mouth and brush against their tongue. While experimenting with a bit of tongue action, don't forget that you should be paying more attention to their lips.

PRESSURE: A good kiss should feel neither like saying goodbye to an elderly relative or being hit in the face with a lust truck. It's all about pressure, or the force applied to the lips. The amount of force you should apply varies according to a number of factors.

THE EQUATION LOOKS LIKE THIS:

LESSON 17B: Kissing

$$PRESSURE = \frac{PASSION \times Situation}{Mood}$$

← a kiss

So let's say you're feeling 10 horny, but you're in a park so that's only a 3 for situation and your partner's feeling a bit gloomy so has a bad mood score of 8. So that's 10 x 3 / 8 = 3.75. That's going to be quite a gentle snog.

Compare that to an evening at home when you've just seen an amazing film and are both feeling horny – that's 10 x 9 / 2 = 45! Game on! Passionate snog a-go-go!

Both types of kiss are GREAT and have their time and place. Not every kiss needs to be a gropey smooch-a-thon. The best boyfriend in the world would have a fantastic repertoire of soft, gentle kisses and hard and horny ones. More to the point he would intuitively know when to deploy each.

If unsure, start slow and build the passion if your other half seems receptive. Attacking a face like a bull in a china shop can be really hot, but it can also be greatly off-putting.

For the sake of EVERYONE IN THE WORLD keep your most passionate kisses to private places. If you insist on noisily licking your partner's face in full public view, I assure you there is a special place in Hades with your name on it.

SALIVA: The goal of a good kiss should not be to deposit as much of your saliva as possible into your partner's mouth. This is why limiting the amount of open-mouthed tongue action is advisable. Similarly, you shouldn't really have to land much more than a delicate frosting to their lips. If you are getting dribble on their chin or cheeks, something is amiss. As long as you remember to swallow during kissing, you should be fine.

Get practising – above all else kissing should be fun. NEVER see kissing purely as an opening act to sex. Sometimes, in the desire for sex, it's easy to neglect kissing, but this is a mistake. The thrill of a first kiss rivals any sex and it's a great way to ease yourself into the idea of a sexual relationship. Enjoy it for what it is. A cheeky snog is a great way to pass the ad breaks on TV, too.

SEX VS LOVE

News flash: you don't have to be in love to have sex. Never heard this before? That's because you've probably been told that, 'when you meet someone, you really, truly love, you will want to share something with them that is SO SPECIAL, a kiss just won't do.' This is true. Your body is the only one you have, so you should look after it the best you can. However it's also true that sex always feels nice, whether you're in love with your partner or not.

Fact

Sometimes, sex is recreational.
That sound you just heard was the thud of prudes hitting the floor as they faint with moral outrage.

So why haven't you heard this before? Well, for one thing, teenage pregnancy rates around the world are too high. Even the most liberal among us acknowledge that having babies as teenagers is far from ideal for you or society. Accidents happen, but no adult is going to encourage you to have loads and loads of wild and free sex for the reasons listed before – babies and sexually transmitted infections.

Also, sex is tied to emotions, no matter what anyone says. There's no such thing as 100 per cent 'no-strings' sex. However hard you might try, feelings always creep in because we ALL WANT TO BE WANTED. Being in a relationship IS the best way to have sex because AFTERWARDS you will feel better about it. All sex involves 'exposing' yourself emotionally and literally to a person. It's much, much less daunting if that person is someone you like, trust and even love.

However, that is in an ideal world. It seems likely, sooner or later, you'll have casual sex. Why? Because not every guy or girl you meet is going to be compatible in terms of a long-term relationship. To employ a weary old cliché – you really do have to kiss a lot of frogs to find your princess or prince.

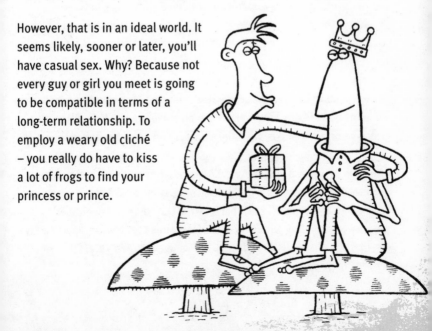

TAKING THE PLUNGE

So you met a girl, or guy, you really like. You dated, you had a snog, you're 'official'. There's a commitment there. Eventually it'll get to the stage where merely kissing your partner is going to feel a tad redundant. Kissing is BRILLIANT and everything, but you might start to want something more. Remember, you'll know you're ready because you will really, really want to have sexyfuntime. If you're content with kissing, then stick with that.

This is perfectly natural and all about the 'curiosity' I mentioned before. The lovely thing about sex in a relationship is that it feels very safe. Not safe from being stabbed or whatever, but safe in that it makes a potentially nerve-wracking situation less so. Think about it – you're naked, you have to perform, you have to not cum in three seconds – there's a lot happening and it's so much better if you KNOW your partner isn't going to laugh at the weird unicorn-shaped mole on your buttock.

Sex is meant to be fun. The best way of ensuring it's fun is by doing it with someone you already have fun with, even someone you love. After all, a girlfriend or boyfriend is basically a best friend you have naked time with.

After millennia, this is still the IDEAL way to have a sexual relationship. A meets B, they date for a while, they have some sex. There are so many benefits to this type of relationship, from the companionship and security to spending whole blissful afternoons together snogging until you literally shrivel up from lack of saliva like a salted slug. (This won't actually happen.)

NO-STRINGS

While being in a committed relationship is the IDEAL way to have sex, you must have by now realised that life doesn't always go the way we want it to. Sometimes you might meet a girl or a guy and think they're hot and you do some dancing and kissing 'in da club' and then in a moment of passion decide to have sex with them. Oh no! Now you will go to Hades!

YOU WON'T.

What will happen is this: you'll wake up the next morning and everything will feel forced and awkward. If you're lucky you'll get a cup of coffee and a bit of toast before being politely shepherded out. THIS IS FINE. You don't have to marry this person, they probably don't want to marry you either. It's unlikely the townspeople will come tearing down the street with flaming torches and pitchforks either. Hopefully you practised safe sex so you have nothing to worry about unduly.

Sometimes all of the above will happen and you'll chat the next morning and realise you met someone really good and three years later you'll get married. These things also happen. Casual sex can become something more.

It's a numbers game. It must be lovely to be the 0.00000001 per cent of couples who end up with their childhood sweetheart. The rest of us, however, need to play the field a bit before scoring a goal. You shouldn't feel GUILTY about doing what comes naturally to all mammals but you should be safe and smart about it.

There may also be times in your life when you just don't WANT to do the whole relationship thing. Having a partner can be fantastic but only if they're the right person. What are you meant to do in the meantime? Luckily there are also guys and girls who are just looking for a bit of fun between boyfriends (or kissing frogs to find a prince). Hurrah! The itch is scratched and fun is had.

There are lots of reasons why you might not want a relationship. Perhaps you're too busy to date, maybe you've just come out of a big relationship, maybe you just can't be bothered. Fact is, sometimes people have casual sex and that is fine as long as you're both HONEST and SAFE. Remember, you don't HAVE to be in a relationship with someone to have sex with them, but you DO need to be honest about it. How would you feel if you woke up next to a super-cute specimen you really wanted to take out to dinner only to find out they didn't really want to date you at all. And, as for being safe, do I seriously need to say it again? Turn to page 111 for more on ALWAYS USING A CONDOM and other safe-sex tips.

NOT HAVING SEX

As mentioned before, there are also times when you might just not feel like sex. There's a lot to be said for waiting until someone really special comes along. A period of celibacy isn't something to be ashamed of. Always better to be picky than sicky when it comes to sex, I feel.

HERE'S THE THING: You know how I just said it was FINE to be celibate, have a sexual relationship or have casual sex? Well it is, but there's a catch. I wonder if I can make it clear.

> # YOU HAVE TO BE 100% HONEST WITH YOUR PARTNER UPFRONT.

Otherwise you run the risk of being a massive lothario dickhead, and we don't want that now, do we? For example if you are feeling like some no-strings sex it wouldn't be very nice to promise the person you're trying to bed a long and healthy relationship, would it? No, it would make you a monstrous shitweasel. Similarly, pretending you don't want a relationship when you do because you're worried it might scare a potential partner off is cowardly.

If everyone was ALWAYS upfront and honest when it came to dating and sex the ice cream industry would go bankrupt in days as no one would have to sit next to a silent phone shovelling Häagen-Dazs in their gob whilst weeping WHY HAVEN'T THEY CALLED?

The only reason to lie is to make yourself look better or because you're scared. Don't be a douchebag. Man up. If you're a big enough boy to have sex, you're big enough to talk about it honestly.

BEING A BOYFRIEND

The jury is still very much out on WHY the animals went into the ark two-by-two given that, in the animal kingdom, nearly ALL mammals are massively into free-love. Only a handful of species mate for life, which is also called being 'monogamous'.

Biologically speaking, it would make far more sense for males to sleep with numerous women – men can make dozens of babies in the time it takes women to have one. Women, again biologically speaking, need a man who is also going to protect and provide for her offspring.

So, it's easy to see why thousands of years since women actually 'needed' men, humans still crave a monogamous relationship. We're genetically programmed to.

MOST OF US SEEM TO DESIRE THE ONE-ON-ONE RELATIONSHIP FOR A NUMBER OF REASONS:

1. **Security:** There is a comfort in knowing there's someone that is just for you, someone who's got your back.

2. **Comfort:** Most relationships come with a degree of cosiness involving sweatpants, DVD boxed sets and take-out food on a Saturday night.

3. **Partnership:** Someone to have adventures with. Someone funny and kind who inspires and supports you to be better.

4. **Love:** Perhaps the most important reason. Love is when you can't be without someone. After 2,000 years and 2,000 hippy poets, no one is any nearer to defining love. For me, it's always looking forward to seeing someone, having a little glow every time you think about them. It takes time to fall in love with someone. At first you see only what the other person is showing you and while you can fall in love with that, you eventually need to fall in love with the real person underneath – all the good bits and bad bits.

5. **Sex on tap:** Self-explanatory. Though not in all cases, of course. If you or your partner chooses abstinence, then this may not apply to your relationship. The best thing about having sex with the same person over and over is that you get REALLY good at it, get to know their body and can try lots of fun new things.

REASONS NOT TO HAVE A RELATIONSHIP

1. **For the sake of it:** The tragic side effect of a culture that thrusts male-female monogamy down our throats is the fact we think this is all there is. There are actually a billion alternatives.

2. **For access to sex:** This brings us back to being HONEST with your partner.

Myth Busting

So many people are in MISERABLE relationships because they think 'this is what humans do'. That's just not true. It is always better to be single and happy than in a bad relationship feeling sad.

Relationships are like buses – sometimes you'll wait at a bus stop for ages, but another one will always rock up eventually. You never know what's just around the corner.

> You can't be a good boyfriend until you've made peace with being single. If you aren't happy being on your own, you'll dive right into the first relationship that turns up ... even if that bus isn't heading in the right direction.

FINDING 'THE ONE'

It's so hard to tell. I know this though: DOUBT is all part of the process. When settling into the relationship, unless you're a moustache-twirling villain, you are basically choosing one partner to the exclusion of all others. How do you know they are 'the one'?

Well here's the thing. When the person's right for you, you'll be having so much fun with them and be so excited to see them that you won't want to see other people. It's TOTALLY NATURAL for other people to catch your eye as you're only human, after all, but you'll think, 'oooh they're hot, but tonight I'm seeing <INSERT NAME>, hurrah!'

Sometimes, the early days are a bit like an addiction, when you just can't get enough of this brilliant new person. It can make you a phone-checking, Facebook-stalking, nail-chewing obsessive. This is also totally normal. I wish more people were honest about new-love-feelings, then we'd all feel a bit less deranged.

THE BOYFRIEND TEST

Now we've done all the groundwork, let's see if you're ready for the real deal. Take the quiz, score yourself and then find out how you did.

1. YOU'VE BEEN ON A FIRST DATE AND IT WENT REALLY WELL. HOW LONG SHOULD YOU WAIT BEFORE YOU TEXT?

a) as the bus pulls away, so they can see you texting from the pavement

b) later that evening to tell them what you're wearing to bed

c) 48 hours later – make them sweat a little

d) you won't need to text them. They're coming home with you, obviously

2. YOU'VE BEEN SEEING SOMEONE FOR A FEW MONTHS WHEN THEIR BIRTHDAY COMES AROUND. WHAT SHOULD YOU GIVE THEM?

a) the most expensive thing you can afford – a Tiffany charm bracelet, an iPad or a trip abroad. The more money you spend the more they will know you love them

b) a handmade card featuring a self-penned poem and thirteen of your own eyelashes

c) a huge box of chocolates and shopping time, because everyone loves shopping, right?

d) a voucher entitling them to five hours of on-demand sex

3. YOUR PARTNER'S DEEPLY IRRITATING BEST FRIEND IS CELEBRATING THEIR BIRTHDAY ON THE SAME DAY YOU HAVE TICKETS FOR A THING YOU REALLY WANT TO DO. DO YOU ...

a) cancel your tickets and go to the birthday party but sulk all night, giving sideways glances and only speaking in monosyllabic grunts?

b) go to your event regardless – it's their best friend, not yours?

c) employ a look-a-like actor to attend the birthday party in your place?

d) ask the friend if they are willing to celebrate their birthday at your prior event?

4. YOU'RE IN A PUBLIC PLACE WHEN A RANDOM STRANGER COMMENTS 'PHWOAR, LOOK AT THE BAPS ON HER'. DO YOU...

a) knock their front teeth out?

b) whip your other half out of the place so fast you wrench their arm from its socket?

c) suggest that your partner may wish to wear less revealing clothing next time?

d) give 'em a squish and say 'yeah, they're all mine, mate'?

5. AFTER DATING FOR SEVERAL WEEKS, YOUR PARTNER INVITES YOU TO A BIG FAMILY WEDDING. YOU'LL FINALLY GET TO MEET THEIR MUM, DAD AND ENTIRE FAMILY. YOU:

a) stock up on industrial strength diarrhoea remedies to combat nerves

b) buy a new suit at once. Mums love you, in fact, your mum is your best friend

c) find an excuse to not go. It's just too much pressure at such an early stage

d) engineer a three-way with your partner and a hot wedding guest

Now add up your scores and you'll see:

MOSTLY AS: You're an ass-hat.

MOSTLY BS: You're a clingy ass-hat.

MOSTLY CS: You're an ass-hat.

MOSTLY DS: You're a pervy ass-hat.

The point of the exercise was to highlight the fact that whether you favour girls or boys, relationships are hard. Really hard. Being single is actually a lot easier than being in a couple because you can be as selfish as you like when you have only yourself to think about.

The key word within relationships is COMPROMISE. This is a fancy word for 'doing stuff you don't want to do'. Unlike CAVING IN, however, it also means you can get your partner to do something they don't want to do by way of revenge. Just kidding!

> **Q: How often is it OK for you to check your partner's texts and emails?**
>
> **A: Erm, never, you controlling psychopath.**
>
> **Similarly it is not OK for them to invade your privacy.**

You do these things for your partner because you care about each other. A good boyfriend will prioritise his lover, which means that the days of doing exactly as you want are numbered.

> **The truest sign of a good boyfriend is one who lets his partner have their own life. A good partner is one who'll let you have a life too.**

BUT HERE'S THE GOOD NEWS:

A. You won't mind this at all because you'll want to see your partner happy. It's alarming how easy it is to put the happiness of others ahead of your own – it's the final part of childish self-centredness we cast off.

B. If you are in a GOOD, HEALTHY relationship, this will work both ways.

What I mean is, you and your partner will allow each other freedom. Only in TERRIBLE relationships are individuality and autonomy tossed aside.

Also, once you're in a settled relationship don't start to neglect your mates. You need balance. One person can't be everything to another – variety is the spice of life, after all. On a serious note, if things go wrong in your relationship, you need to know your mates will still be there to look after you.

Domestic Violence

This should go without saying: violent relationships are a BIG no-no. Men should never, ever hit women. Women should never, ever hit men. Same-sex couples must never hit each other either. It is never acceptable. If it were happening to your best friend or mum, what would you say to them? Hurting someone emotionally or physically is WRONG.

No violent, abusive, angry relationship is worth salvaging. There are MILLIONS of partners out there who won't attack you or make you feel like dog poo – shag one of them instead.

If we look at the examples from the quiz, a bit of cheeky compromise could have saved the day. Take the 'best friend's birthday' question. If you bought your tickets to the THING first, it's pretty unreasonable of your partner to expect to throw away a small fortune when they could quite easily go to the party by themselves. A good partner would say, 'you have fun and take lots of pictures so I can see what it was like', and you would say, 'tell your friend I'm sorry and that I hope they have a lovely birthday, buy them a drink on me.'

As with sex, communication is key. Screaming, shouting, bickering, jealousy and emotional blackmail have no place in a healthy relationship.

If you have siblings, you'll know that all rules are off when you fight. There is no blow too low or dirty and all ammunition is fair game. This can become true in relationships. You'll learn which buttons to press to really piss your partner off and get your own way. Don't go there. A few disagreements are inevitable, as is a whole bunch of compromise, but treat a partner the same way you would a friend. Would you scream and shout and throw crockery? I should hope not. Refer back to the previous advice: No relationship is better than a bad relationship. A girlfriend or boyfriend is meant to be the BEST thing in your life, not the worst.

KEEPING LOVE ALIVE

After the initial rush of a new relationship has worn off, it's important to do everything possible to keep your love fresh and exciting. Never take your partner for granted.

Let your partner know you care. This is easily done in a text message. Post funny pics on their Facebook wall. Let them know if you're running late. Never stop complimenting your partner. When real life kicks in it's easy to complain and moan, but MAKE THE EFFORT to be positive every day.

THE STICKY SOLUTION SOLVER

HER	YOU	NEVER
DOES MY BUM LOOK BIG IN THIS?	YOUR BUTT LOOKS AMAZING IN THAT.	IT DOES A BIT, YEAH.
DO YOU LIKE MY NEW HAIR?	YEAH, IT REALLY SUITS YOUR FACE-SHAPE.	HAVE YOU HAD IT CUT?
IS SHE PRETTIER THAN ME?	YOU'RE COMPLETELY DIFFERENT BUT I PREFER YOU.	FACIALLY, YES.
DO YOU THINK I NEED TO LOSE WEIGHT?	ONLY IF YOU WANT TO - YOU LOOK GREAT.	WHAT'S THAT, JABBA?
DO YOU LIKE THIS OUTFIT?	YEAH - YOU LOOK A BIT LIKE <INSERT FILM STAR NAME>.	NO, YOU LOOK LIKE A DRAG QUEEN THAT GOT DRESSED QUICKLY IN A DARKENED CHARITY SHOP.

Note it'd be easiest to answer any of these questions with 'Do YOU think ... ?' but that is infuriating and looks like you're dodging the issue. An unsolicited compliment is always better than an elicited one.

IF THERE WERE A RECIPE FOR A PERFECT BOYFRIEND IT'D PROBABLY GO SOMETHING LIKE THIS:

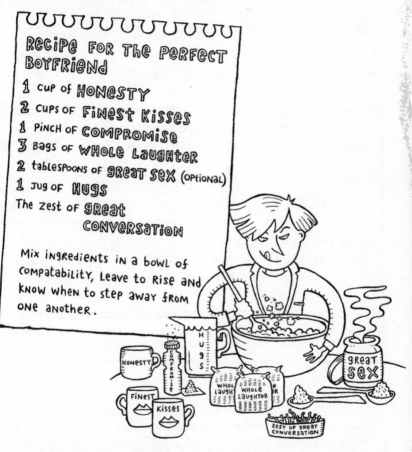

Recipe for the Perfect Boyfriend

1 cup of HONESTY
2 cups of FINEST KISSES
1 pinch of COMPROMISE
3 bags of WHOLE LAUGHTER
2 tablespoons of GREAT SEX (optional)
1 jug of HUGS
The zest of GREAT CONVERSATION

Mix ingredients in a bowl of compatability, leave to rise and know when to step away from one another.

Relationships are hard, and they take work, but the right relationship is totally worth it. However not everyone is compatible – sometimes that's even harder to admit.

TIME TO SAY GOODBYE

Almost as vital as the start of a relationship is its end. Yes, I know, this is bleak, but everything ends, and few relationships end in convenient simultaneous death like in *The Notebook*. Sooner or later, one of you may want to want to walk off into the sunset.

This isn't a bad thing. I blame Cinderella and 'Happy Ever After'. We never saw the part where Cinderella realised Prince Charming was incapable of change and started to have feelings for the handsome groomsman.

Everything changes. Sometimes couples change and the change suits them both and they grow old and grey together. For many of us though, as your needs change your partner might have different needs so you'll want to go in separate directions. I think we should stop saying that relationships that end are 'failed' and simply say that 'we changed'. A relationship is only 'failing' if two people better apart stay together.

There are a multitude of reasons why a relationship might end. Observe figure d.

CHEATI NG

This is a tricky one. People define cheating differently. Are you allowed to chat to an ex on Facebook? For some people that would be cool, but it might drive others mad. Kissing and doing sex with someone that's not your partner is nearly always frowned on. You'll note though, that having

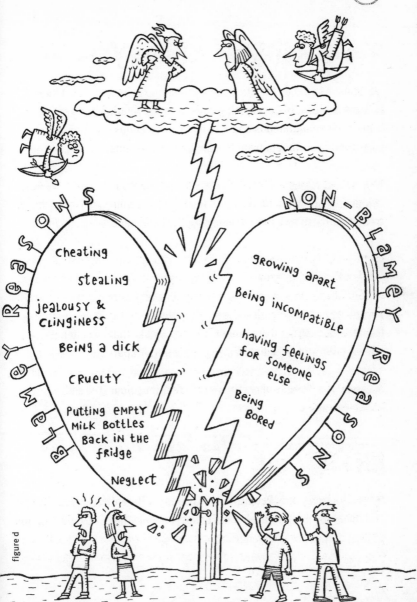

figured

feelings for someone else is on the 'non-blame' list. Why? Because sometimes you can't help it – you don't have to act on it though.

It is a question of trust. Invading someone's private text messages or e-mails isn't fair and is only a hop, skip and a jump from donning a wig and sunglasses and following your partner around all day. If you truly think your partner is up to no good you have to – drumroll – ASK THEM. If they deny it and you still have suspicions, why? What about them is suspicious or is it really you needing to be in control? If you can't trust what your partner is saying is true then why are you with them at all?

THE DUMP

If you've been seeing someone for more than a couple of dates and you want out, it's VITAL that you end things properly. In the chapter on dating, I encouraged you to man up and explain if you don't want a second date. This is the ONLY circumstance where's it forgivable to do the 'just don't call' tactic. If you haven't heard from a date after 48 hours or so, we can all assume there isn't going to be a follow-up, I think.

Anything more than a couple of dates and you MUST do it properly. Regard figure e.

Here's the thing. Breaking up with someone is potentially explosive. Choosing any method from column two is only likely to throw in another stick of dynamite. You'll get this:

'YOU'RE DUMPING ME BY E-MAIL? YOU ARE SUCH A DICK!'

Whereas it could have just been:

'YOU'RE DUMPING ME?'

Yes, it'll still sting, but doing it properly softens the blow considerably.

figure e

I know you're probably thinking, 'Gee, Gramps, get with twenty-first century ... everyone dumps people on Facebook', but manners never date. Even if you can get away with sending a well-worded text, it's still BETTER to do it in person. The only reason not to is because you're scared and it's awkward. WELL BOO-HOO – GET OVER IT. If you do it properly, they'll go back into the world with a much better impression of you and, importantly, won't be going all over town and the Internet saying, 'THIS GUY IS A TOTAL SHITWEASEL.'

GOODIES AND BADDIES

Any graduate from the Cliché University will tell you that you can't make an omelette without breaking a few eggs. I'm afraid the same is true of hearts. As much as we try to follow all the rules and treat people with respect, at some point, inevitably, you're going to upset people. Yep, sooner or later, you're going to be a villain in someone else's internal soap opera.

In many ways it's easier to be DUMPED than it is to be the DUMPER because, when someone dumps you, you get to be a fantastically sympathetic victim.

Friends will rally around you with ice-cream ...

FRIEND: 'You were WAY TOO GOOD for him/her, hun – they'll never meet someone as good as you.
YOU: *WAIL*.

As the dumper, you are more evil than Satan at a rock concert.

While no one wants to be a villain, you shouldn't let this stop you from having those difficult conversations or ending a relationship if it doesn't fit properly. Another cliché – dumping someone should be like pulling off a plaster – it will hurt, but fleetingly. Avoiding awkward moments, or trying to shitweasel your way out of a relationship by ignoring texts or faking relocation to Yemen will succeed only in making you a bigger baddie.

Dumping people is AWFUL, but every once in a while, you'll have to accept your villainous crown of skulls and get on with it.

A HANDY SCRIPT

Choose a venue: I suggest a public place because they will be less likely to flip out. Their home will do, but not yours. Kicking someone out after you've dumped them is shady. Make sure you are nowhere too quiet or too noisy.

• If you've said 'we need to talk', they'll already know what's coming.

• Don't try to make it better than it is. If you want out do not offer false hope by saying, 'I need a break', or, ' I need some time to think'. If you really do want some time to think, this is fine, but do set a timescale e.g. 'Let's meet in a week and talk again.'

- Always stick to I FEEL/I THINK statements rather than placing blame. For example: 'I know you've been carrying on with the pizza delivery guy and I FEEL that's unacceptable'.

- Otherwise, it's over to you to explain why you want out of the relationship. For instance: 'I'm so sorry to do this, but this just isn't working for me.' You need to give more detail than this, however. 'You're lovely, but I feel we don't have that much in common – I'm not sure we have any shared interests.'

Do you see how that's quite difficult to argue with? Your partner might rattle off a list, but you can stick to, 'I FEEL this is not the case.'

> **Never, ever say 'it's not you, it's me', unless you want a drink in your face.**

- Very often it's really hard to vocalise what's wrong with a relationship, it just feels off somehow. This is where it gets tricky, because you really do have to give a reason and, 'I think I can do better than you', is likely to go down as well as bird flu at a poultry farm.

There's nothing wrong with: 'I'm so sorry about this, but I'm just not enjoying this. It's nothing you've done – perhaps my head's just not in the right place for a relationship at the moment.' Again, argue with that. In these situations, I often find the other person is WELL AWARE that something is off and will likely agree.

- If your partner IS disappointed and upset do NOT back down purely because you feel bad. Offering false hope is a terrible thing to do. Likewise, only say, 'let's be friends', if you actually want to be friends. Grey areas can be very confusing. NEVER sleep with someone once you've dumped them, because this only makes grey areas murkier.

- Make the meeting a proper ending. Don't say, 'let's get together soon', if you don't mean it. Go away with a, 'look after yourself. I'll see you around.'

- If the other person starts down the heartbroken text/e-mail/call route, be aware this is most likely an attempt to get you back. You should respond to these politely, but you're no longer obliged to them if you've ended things properly. Be kind, but stay firm. If the theme is 'let's give it another go', say, 'That's not what I want, and I think we should both move on.'

The horror of a bad break-up may be enough to make you never want another relationship ever again. If everyone behaves with a degree of maturity, however, a break-up, although sad can be clean.

FIRST AID FOR THE DUMPED

What if it's you that got dumped? As you can see, when the situation is reversed it's never nice, but there's actually nothing you can do about it. Nothing at all. What are you thinking? You'll beg your way back into their heart? Unlikely.

You are allowed a right to reply. Sticking with our I FEEL statements, you can say, 'I feel we have a good relationship that is worth sticking with. I believe we'll regret it if we give up.' They might agree, but if they don't you have to let them go. You have to move on.

This is going to hurt. It will hurt for two reasons:

1. You will miss them.

2. It's not what you want and we ALL like getting our own way.

The sooner we accept that things might not go our way, the happier we'll be. Wanting things we can't have is a horrid toxic-belly feeling, so the sooner you can identify it and treat it like the inner spoiled brat it is, the happier you will be.

Regarding the first point, it will get better with time – AWFUL-BUT-TRUE CLICHÉ-ALERT). It might take quite a lot of time. There are people I still miss, even years later, because every time you fall in love it's unique to that person. That said, over time it fades to almost nothing, and when someone new comes along (and someone new always does) they are brighter and more exciting, completely taking over your head. Basically it's like when the iPhone 5 came out. It totally pissed all over the iPhone 4.

If you're feeling super-sad, talk to someone you trust. At some point everyone goes through a bad break-up and everyone survives more or less intact.

WHATEVER YOU DO, DON'T BEG!

CHAPTER 7

BEING A MAN

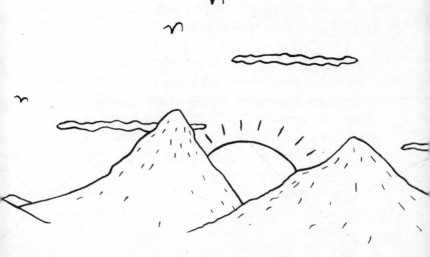

BEING A MAN

I wish I could tell you that the day you turn 20, a glorious tide of wisdom will flood your head. In fact, I'm afraid it gets no easier once you throw in the added complication of a career. However, I have found that as soon as you leave school, everything changes. You're off the leash and everything that happened at school, whether you were an insouciant lion or tragic vole, is immediately forgotten. You get a fresh start.

Adult life is only different to adolescent life in that you suddenly get an unprecedented increase in your number of choices. For most of us, our early lives are free of choice, with most being made by our parents or carers. Suddenly being free to make your own choices can be daunting and you'll certainly make some mistakes.

It is these choices that will form the sort of man you will become. A choice to sleep until noon is unlikely to see you enter a fulfilling career. A choice to drink or take drugs to excess or tattoo your face with swearwords will be similarly limiting. If you look at ANY successful person in ANY field you like, the thing they will have in common is that they all made difficult choices and sacrifices.

Professional sportspeople have dragged themselves out of bed at 5am to train every day since they were young kids. Actors, dancers and

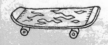

singers passed hanging out at the local bus shelter to rehearse. Writers and novelists write because they love it, not because they have JK Rowling's bank balance.

This message is oddly missing from school. Teachers give you work, but don't tell you why. The truth is this, teachers make you work at school because anything worth having in life will take WORK.

Sadly, crap reality TV has led you to believe that anyone can be rich and famous overnight. This is a lie. I know some of the people who make reality TV shows and those 'accidentally' famous people are also getting up at 5am to film. Basically, there is no such thing as an easy path to fortune. You have to WORK. It's worth it though. It'll take some time and a crushing lack of sleep most likely, but eventually, if you can identify what you love doing in life, adulthood can be fantastic.

Another thing you rarely hear is: do what you want. You might not make any money doing it, but don't let that stop you. If you want to paint, paint. Yeah, you might have to work in a paperclip factory during the day, but you can ALWAYS paint in the evening. This applies to anything. If it's something you love, you'll find a way.

It's not only your time you have to make choices with. As an adult you have choices with your relationships too. As a child you were 'put' with your peers and often 'told' who your friends are. As you edge towards adulthood, you'll realise that you have more in common with some people than others. You'll phase some friends out as you make new, like-minded chums.

Your ideas, opinions, politics and beliefs will solidify. You might find that these are very different to those of your family and friends. Sometimes it feels a little like the blinkers have been removed and you're finally seeing the world with your own eyes.

I believe there are three stages of awareness:

1. Realising your friends can be dicks.

2. Realising your parents can be dicks.

3. Realising that you can be a dick.

The slow realisation that your parents or carers aren't superheroes but are, in fact as messed up as the rest of the world, can be disheartening. That is, until you reach stage three and realise everyone is struggling with the real world. The only reason you may not have struggled is because your adults were protecting you. Now you're on your own.

These choices also extend to your sexual relationships. Once you've got all those first kisses and first sexual experiences out of the way, bigger questions such as, 'do I want to spend my life with this person?', will start to enter your head. You may eventually start to think about marriage and children, even if it's to rule them out. You guessed it, there are infinite choices to be made.

Do you want kids? Do you even LIKE kids? The idea that we all HAVE to get married and have kids is considered deeply old fashioned now.

World travel isn't as exotic as it once was – are you the sort of person who wants to explore the world? Some people never put down roots. Some people can't wait to. You don't have to follow the path your parents, carers, friends, brothers or sisters took.

Not long ago, pretty much EVERYONE went to university. It was becoming the done thing. That's changing, with hideous student debts and no guarantee of a career post study, people are looking for alternative paths into the workplace. Do what feels right for you.

You get to CHOOSE what sort of man you want to be. Do you want to be the sort of man that treats people badly? Do you want to be the sort of man who sees people's differences before he sees the similarities? Do you want to be a man people respect, or a man people are scared of?

Remember this. Every time you interact with someone, even for the briefest of moments, every shopkeeper, every passer-by, you leave a fingerprint. You make an impression everywhere you go. What do you want that impression to be? Kind, friendly, approachable? Aloof, dismissive, frosty? Warm, funny, charming? Loutish, obnoxious, noisy? Everywhere you go, every person you meet ...

Sometimes it's exhausting. It's early in the morning and you just want your effing hazelnut latte and the coffee person is all, 'Cheer up, love, it might never happen'. It's easier to give them the stink eye but that barista will quite rightly assume you are a massive, massive wanker. The next time you go in, she will think, 'brilliant, it's that wanker'. Everywhere you go, everyone you meet ...

On the top deck of a bus, you are with five friends so you feel invincible. You're playing music out of your phone knowing full well it's going to annoy the other commuters. Guess what? It's intimidating and annoying. In that moment you're representing every young person and adding to the myth that ALL young adults are noisy and loutish, which just isn't true. Everywhere you go, everyone you meet ...

A girl chats to you 'in da club' and you're rude and dismissive. She will talk to her friends, who will talk to their friends. Everywhere you go, everyone you meet ...

The man you become is a collage of people's opinions of you but the good news is you get to decide what people think of you. Send the right messages about yourself and the world will see that man.

I do hope this book hasn't terrified you. However many books you read, however much advice you seek, none of us can hold back time. Like it or not, we're all getting older and constantly changing. At puberty the change is self-evident but the truth is you'll never, ever stop. The man you are at 20 will be different to the one you are at 30. To adopt a much-overused cliché: It really is a journey. I like to think of us as modelling clay, constantly being moulded and squished by our experiences.

Change is inevitable, so we might as well welcome it. Ask yourself every day, 'Am I having fun?' Being a man should be fun – life goes a LOT faster than you think. Enjoy.

THE SCHOOL DICTIONARY

As if school isn't hard enough, there is NOTHING worse than not knowing what everyone's talking about. What's worse, what if people are making up plausible sounding terms and asking if you like them?

'Hey, are you into doinking?' What do you say? Is doinking a great thing that ALL the cool kids are doing or is it filthy and disgusting? OH GOD, KILL ME NOW.

Help is at hand. There now follows a glossary of vaguely sexual terms you might overhear. Obviously there's a new one every week so if in doubt, just make a semi-vague face of aloofness and say, 'Uh. No. Lame.' Even if it's a cool thing, you can pretend it's SO LAST WEEK. We talked about this earlier – I reckon about 90 per cent of what you hear at school is total bollocks, but some of the things in the list can be fun in a CONSENSUAL relationship.

Blow job
Oral sex, note involves no actual blowing

Bondage/S&M
The kinky art of tying up/restraining a willing sexual partner

Crabs
A marine crustacean OR another term for pubic lice

Crywank
A sad wank

Cock
A penis or a male chicken

Cunniligus
Oral sex on a woman

Cum
Informal term for semen/sperm

Dick
A word to describe a penis OR someone called Richard

Dildo
A sex toy to insert in the front-bum OR bum-bum

DILF
Dad I'd like to f*ck

Douching
Washing out a body cavity such as the vagina or anus

DP
Double penetration – two willies one hole OR simultaneous penetration of vagina and anus. ONLY in porn.

Eating out
Cunnilingus. Actually means eating IN if you think about it

Face Handies
A blow-job

Flaps
Unflattering term for a woman's labia minora

Flick the bean
Female masturbation, notably stimulation of the clitoris

Golden Shower
Weeing on a consenting partner or allowing them to wee on you

Handies
A more charming way of describing masturbation

Jizz
Another word for cum (semen)

Meat Curtains
Another unflattering term for a woman's labia minora

MILF
Mum I'd like to f*ck

Motorboating
Making an engine noise between a woman's breasts

One-Night Stand / NSA.
No-strings-attached OR one-night-stand sex

Pussy
A slang term for a woman's bits

Rimming
A term that means licking your partner's (clean) anus

Scat
Eating poop (sad face)

Spooge
Another word for cum (semen)

Spooning
Cuddling (or having sex) with one partner lying behind the other

Spunk
Another word for cum (semen)

Titwank
A handie administered between breasts

V-Card
'Membership card' to the 'VIRGINITY CLUB'

Vibrator
Vibrating sex toy

Windmilling
When a woman swooshes her breasts in a circular motion

> When writing *Being A Boy* I called on other 'PSAs' (Puberty Surviving Adults) as well as focus groups in schools. These interviews were conducted in the summer of 2012.

SYNONYMS FOR 'PENIS'

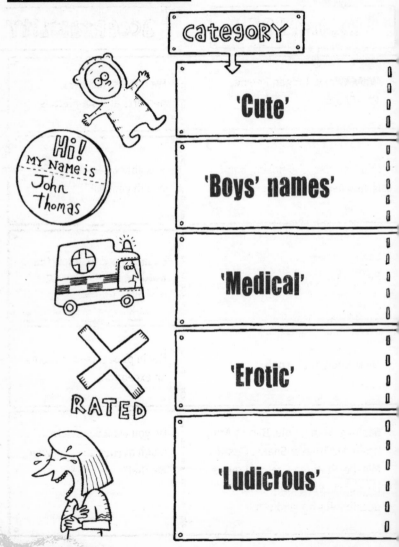

category

'Cute'

'Boys' names'

'Medical'

'Erotic'

'Ludicrous'

examples	acceptability
Willy, Winky, Todger, Peenie, Pee-Pee	For babies, toddlers, perverts and simpletons
John Thomas, Thompson, Ralph, Little ‹insert your name›, Frank	Possibly when discussing it with your GP
Penis, Member	Usually used to follow the word 'severed'. These are NOT sexy words.
Dick, Cock, Tool, Knob	Not in public. Locker rooms an exception.
Schlong, Wang, Pole, Baby's Arm, One-eyed Trouser Snake, Gristle-Missile, Stationery related terms i.e. pencil, Pork Sword. The possibilities are endless.	Do you want women to laugh at your dick? Answer me that?

BANNED WORDS

Banned because they are only ever used against women.

FACT: both men AND women get horny.

FACT: both men and women are allowed to have casual sex without judgement.

SLUT

SLAG

WENCH

WHORE

FLOOZY

HO

SLAPPER

HARLOT

TRAMP

TART

HELPFUL NUMBERS AND STUFF

Useful websites and numbers for you to know:

ABUSE AND BULLYING

Childline: 0800 1111

Anti-Bullying Alliance: http://www.anti-bullyingalliance.org.uk/

Cyber-bullying: http://www.thinkuknow.co.uk/11_16/

DRUGS AND ALCOHOL

Talk to Frank: www.talktofrank.com

Drink Aware: www.drinkaware.co.uk

MENTAL HEALTH, ANXIETY AND DEPRESSION

Young Minds: www.youngminds.org.uk

Teen Mental Health: www.teenmentalhealth.org

(OR see your family doctor).

SEX

Bish Blog (for guidance on sex, porn and contraception – over 16s): http://bishuk.com/

Brook Young People's Clinic (Contraception, STIs and abortion): http://www.brook.org.uk/

Find NHS Sexual Health services (including GUM clinics) near you: http://www.nhs.uk/servicedirectories

The Site (for advice on sex, drugs, families and careers): http://www.thesite.org/

BEING A GROWN-UP

Thank you for buying this book for your offspring or youthful ward. Straight away this makes you a concerned and caring individual. Why? Because being a boy is harder than it looks. However much you've told a boy YOU CAN TALK TO ME ABOUT ANYTHING, some things are really hard to say.

Our society tells us that some of the things in this book are RUDE or DIRTY or NAUGHTY when, in fact, the vast majority of them are utterly unavoidable. You can't run away from biological destiny and you can't shield young people from the world, so STEP AWAY FROM THE COTTON-WOOL-LINED BIOSPHERE. If a boy is told things are dirty, he won't feel comfortable talking about them I'm afraid.

You might think there are bits in this book where I've GONE TOO FAR or CROSSED THE LINE, but here's the truth:

NONE OF US GREW UP WITH BROADBAND.

We will never, ever know what it is like to have high quality pornography delivered to our mobile phones as a ten year old. THIS is the reality of what is happening. More and more young people are having their introduction to sex education this way. The porn that's likely to be passed around on a school bus isn't going to be NICE, soft, fluffy porn, if there is such a thing. It'll be raw and raunchy.

These pornographic images are confusing and scary for both young men and women. Imagine if you saw that and thought, 'holy crap is

THAT what sex is?' I worry a lot of young men are wrongly learning that all sex involves fetishes and is brutal. The problem is this: schools can't actually SHOW sexual intercourse so what they see online is more graphic and detailed than what your child would learn in school.

It is my hope that this book will bridge the gap between what teachers can discuss in schools and what your child will have already witnessed, or will probably witness in the near future online. If you think you've protected your child from the evils of the Internet, I'd argue you are deluding yourself as the more taboo something is, the more a young person will seek it out. We were all young once – you remember what it was like. That curiosity is natural. Let's scaffold teenage sexuality, not battle it.

For eight years I was a teacher specialising in PSHCE, or 'personal, social, health and citizenship education'. It was my job to ensure that sex education was taught to a high level. I've delivered sex education many times to many young people. As a full-time writer, I still spend a lot of time in schools talking to young adults and I hope I can communicate in a way that is appropriate and appealing to this age group.

There is nothing in this book that your child won't have heard on the playground. At best though, he's probably heard half a story or inaccurate gossip. It's my goal to present the FACTS in a very un-sensational manner. *Being a Boy* is not a sexy book. It is a book about sex. There is nothing titillating in these pages.

Anything in this book you might think is shocking, I guarantee he has already heard and seen much worse.

Hopefully, by providing a warts-and-all account of sex and relationships, your young person will be less likely to truffle for answers online, and will hopefully set his friends straight when they present him with horror stories.

As well as the biology of sex and puberty I have also tackled issues surrounding bullying and relationships. I think we all understand that 'boyfriends and girlfriends' can make an already difficult social situation even harder, so hopefully there is advice here that will light the way. When I was at school, boys talked about sex constantly, but we NEVER talked about our anxieties surrounding sex. I hope there is a level of emotional literacy that young men can take away from this book.

There are so many things that should be taught in schools but aren't. How to chat someone up, how to talk about contraception, how to dump someone properly. It's no wonder we all make such a mess of life when we're young.

It's also worth noting that PSHCE is NOT mandatory in schools, so provision varies wildly between schools. It's a lottery as to whether your child is receiving ANY of these positive, healthy messages. The final aim of the book therefore is to foster better, healthier relationships between young people – be they sexual or not. I was lucky enough in my career to work with the EXCEPTIONAL Healthy Schools Team in Brighton & Hove and they were able to advise me as I wrote to make sure that this book is BANG UP-TO-DATE with what is being taught in schools AND in line with government advice. I also worked with young people in London schools who provided most of the starting points in the text and all of the FAQs and acted as my research group for this book. Yep, they really do talk A LOT about sex, I'm afraid.

I heartily encourage you to read this book alongside your young person. If successful it'll give you something to talk about, or at the very least you'll get a valuable glimpse into his world right now. Teenage boys being teenage boys, you might have to lead him to this book – after all a book about sex and puberty is potentially cringe-tastic. This is why I've tried to make it funny. I'm not being standoffish or glib about these important issues, I've simply sugared the pill. There are some life lessons in here, but I don't want it to feel like homework.

Go on, leave it on the side of his bed. The word SEX is featured. He'll pick it up eventually.

THANK YOUS

This book more than most, was a collaboration so there are lots of people to thank.

In no particular order: Jo Williamson, Martina Challis, Russell McLean, Tori Kosara and ALL at Red Lemon Press.

Particular thanks to Sam Beal and all the pupils I've taught for all their challenging questions! The First Story group at Lambeth Academy.

To Patrick, thank you for the discussion on 'willy waggling' that found its way into the book. Man, that sounds dodgy.

Personal thanks to Sam Powick, Nic Strachan, Kat Dare, Stuart Powick, Neil Palmer, Niall Caverly, Tom Jackman and all the friends who shared their horror stories.

ABOUT THE AUTHOR

For eight years, James Dawson was a teacher specialising in Personal, Social, Health and Citizenship Education (PSHCE). His main remit was ensuring that these subjects were taught to a high standard across several schools. He collaborated on projects involving bullying, sex education, drugs and alcohol education and family diversity.

He now writes full-time and lives in London. His debut, best-selling YA novel *Hollow Pike*, was nominated for the prestigious Queen of Teen prize, and was followed by publication of the YA thriller *Cruel Summer* in 2013.

When he's not writing books to scare teenagers in a variety of different ways, James is busy listening to pop music and watching *Doctor Who* and horror movies.

You can find him on:
twitter: @_jamesdawson
Facebook: facebook.com/jamesdawsonbooks